OFF-ROAD

OFF-ROAD RUNNING

Sarah Rowell

The Crowood Press

First published in 2002 by
The Crowood Press Ltd
Ramsbury, Marlborough
Wiltshire SN8 2HR

www.crowood.com

© Sarah Rowell 2002

British Library Cataloguing-in-Publication Data
A catalogue record for this book is available from the British Library.

ISBN 1 86126 523 9

All photographs by Peter Hartley, except photograph on page 124,
by John Coon.

Typeset by Textype, Cambridge

Printed and bound in Great Britain by Bookcraft, Midsomer Norton

Contents

DEDICATION

To Cliff and Ken.

ACKNOWLEDGEMENTS

As usual with a book like this there are a host of people who consciously or sub-consciously have contributed and deserve acknowledgement.

To those who were persuaded to read a chapter or two, your comments, however critical, really were much appreciated and I owe you a pint.

A big thanks also to those who gave permission for their expertise to be 'borrowed': Dr Andy Jones, Ms Jane Griffin, Dr Richard Budgett, Prof Dave Collins and Mr Martin Bagness. It is always better coming from the experts.

To the runners in the six case studies: thanks for your time and your secrets.

Finally thanks to all those who I have run with, tried to help run faster, or talked running with, and those who have tried to help me run faster or have patched me up to enable me to continue running.

ABOUT THE AUTHOR

Sarah Rowell is a runner. She had a fleeting international career in the early 1980s, including competing in the first women's Olympic marathon in 1984 and clocking 2.28.06 for a British marathon record in 1985. Subsequent sciatic nerve related problems meant an end to road and track racing, but not off-road running. Over the last fifteen years Sarah has and continues to tackle all the disciplines covered by this book, sometimes internationally, sometimes not quite so successfully. Despite her achievements on the road she rates her favourite moment as winning the 1986 off-road Seven Sisters Marathon outright, in a time that has to date only ever been beaten by one man.

A sports scientist by profession, Sarah completed her PhD looking at running injuries. She now works as a consultant in high performance sport and is a regular contributor to *Running fitness* magazine and other publications.

Forewords

There is nobody in these islands who has proved to be a master of so many branches of atheletics as Sarah Rowell. In the 1980s she ran a brilliant London Marathon in a world-class time of under 2hr 30min and then went on to win the Seven Sisters Marathon over a tough course on the South Downs, beating all the men. The record she set that day was not beaten by anyone, man or woman, for many a year. And then she took to the mountains and proved to be equally brilliant.

All this practical experience has been allied to her training as a Sports Scientist – that is what makes this book so unique. And 'unique' is the right word because only Sarah has the wisdom to combine the scientific knowledge of someone who holds a PhD with the experience of a world-class performer.

Chris Brasher CBE
Olympic Gold medallist
in the steeplechase
Founder and first Chairman
of the British Orienteering Federation
Founder of the London Marathon
and the Brasher Boot company

As a serious, but maybe not so talented runner, I used to experiment with my training, my diet and my lifestyle in order to try to find that crucial edge over my opponents. Now I use that knowledge and experience to help the athletes I coach to find the right balance and training mix to fulfil their potential, and hopefully their goals while having fun at the same time.

These are things that this book can help you achieve. In writing *Off-Road Running* Sarah has combined her knowledge and expertise of how to train to get the best out of yourself, with practical experience of the various forms of off-road running.

Think of the first part of the book as a coach, one who can help challenge you to get the best out of yourself. While the second part provides you with the insider knowledge to be able get the most out of running off-road – whether that's successfully tackling a mountain race or simply making the most of your local countryside.

Having known Sarah, followed her career and had innumerable running conversations with her, often over a beer, during the last twenty years it is a great pleasure to see her passing on her vast knowledge and experience to others in a very readable and practical way.

Alan Storey
UK Athletics Endurance High
Performance Coach
Coach to numerous medal winners at
Olympic, World & European Championships
and Commonwealth Games.

Introduction

Many people run, for many different reasons. Ever since the running boom of the early 1980s, running has been socially acceptable, no longer the preserve of a few strange, mainly male, beings. The odd thing about the 1980s' trend was not that everyone seemed to want to run marathons, but that everything was geared around running on the roads.

More recently the trend has shifted and as if by magic the proponents of running – magazines and shoe companies – have discovered what many have known for a long time, which is that running off-road has plenty going for it. Not only is it considered to be better for your bones and joints, there is also less pollution, together with fewer traffic worries, more variety and normally better scenery. OK, so there is also more mud, a greater chance of being stung, the odd stile or gate to overcome and the prospect of unusual animal encounters. Off-road running has tests of its own and is usually more fun.

As runners look for new challenges, road races face ever greater pressure; competing, not just running off-road, is increasing in popularity. That is what this book is all about, helping you in your quest, not just to run off-road, but also to race off-road, and to race well. If you are new to off-road running, or if you want to try a different discipline, or if you are looking for new training ideas or that extra edge, then this book is for you.

I have aimed to combine a background in sports science and high performance sport with twenty years' experience of running and competing off-road to provide a practical and informative text, based on experience and underpinned by science.

The book falls naturally into two parts. Chapters 1 to 4 cover the training basics relevant to all forms of off-road running. Do not, however, expect to find detailed training programmes for you to follow slavishly. Training programmes should be very personal things, and therefore who better to design them than the person they are for? This is not to devalue coaches, as good coaches work on the same principle of developing individual training programmes for their runners. This book is about helping you to help yourself develop your own training based on sound principles.

Chapters 5 to 10 each cover one of the types of off-road running. While there will inevitably be some degree of overlap (when, for example, does a hard trail race become a fell race?), each chapter looks in more detail at the specific requirements of a particular discipline, as well as giving practical advice and sneaky tips to help give you the confidence to tackle new running challenges.

That is it. Enjoy, and I hope the book helps you to get as much fun, enjoyment and satisfaction from running off-road as I do.

Sarah Rowell

CHAPTER ONE
Planning Your Training

INTRODUCTION

For many people running is about going out of the front door and doing just that: running. Where they run, how far, how fast and how hard depends on how they feel at that moment. If this is your approach, then it will help you to stay fit, healthy and hopefully happy, but if you want to improve or set yourself challenging goals, then some degree of planning and structure will be needed for your training.

The easy option is to follow one of the many training programmes published in running books and magazines. These could be likened to 'off the peg' clothes – great if you are of average or normal proportions, but who is? Much better is to understand the basic training principles that underpin what you should be doing. This will enable you to then either adapt published training programmes to fit your unique circumstances, or go the whole way and design your own 'bespoke' training programme. If you decide to do the latter, then it is important to remember two things. Firstly, never stop learning. Other runners, magazines and books are all great sources of new ideas for training, which you can then adapt to suit you, as is every training session you do: 'each run is a lesson' (Mike Boit). Secondly, be inventive. Once you have grasped the basic principles of training, the only limit to the number and variety of training sessions is your own imagination. One well-known endurance coach is renowned for never giving his

athletes the same track session twice. Not only does this help prevent monotony and boredom, but also stops athletes comparing their times over different sessions, when it is likely that the background to each session is different. Other coaches and athletes prefer to have regular training sessions which can be used to gauge improvement.

Finally, contrary to what some would like you to believe, there are no right or wrong training sessions, only bad training programmes. One thing that becomes apparent if you look at the various training programmes used by elite runners is that, while following the basic training principles, they are all different. The key point is that you must work out the approach that works best for you.

The following sections will give you the background required in order to put together your own training programme.

> 'The thinking must be done first before training begins'
>
> Peter Coe

TRAINING PRINCIPLES

Underpinning all training, whatever the sport, are the following core training principles.

Progressive Overload

Our bodies can be quite clever things at times, adapting within reason to the environment in which they are placed and the stresses placed on them. Regular overload of the body's various physiological systems (by training) helps bring about adaptive changes at a cellular level. This in turn results in super-compensation which enables the body to cope with the load (or training) placed on it.

Once this point is reached it is time to increase the training load again, in order to re-stress the body and to continue the process of improvement. Increasing training does not just mean increasing the number of sessions per day or per week; rather it can be adjusted in a number of interrelated ways:

- increasing the volume: how much you train (i.e. increasing the number of miles or hours);
- increasing the intensity: how hard you train (i.e. increasing the speed at which you run or, if doing speed work, decreasing the recovery time between efforts); or
- increasing the frequency: how often you train (i.e. increasing the number of days on which you train or the number of sessions).

These will be considered in more detail in Chapter 3.

Rest

When you train you place a stress on the body, but it is during the subsequent rest and recovery that the resultant physiological adaptations to the training take place, leading to increases in fitness. Appropriate rest and recovery are therefore an essential part of any training programme. Getting the balance right is an art in itself. Too much rest and the training stimulus is unlikely to be great enough to cause positive changes in fitness. Too little rest and the time available to the body to enable it to recover and adapt is not enough, resulting in, at best, poor performance or, at worst, injury, illness or

breakdown. Ideally the best form of rest and recovery is actual rest, not pottering about, doing other sports, doing the shopping and cleaning and so on. However, for most of us these activities all have to be fitted in to our weekly timetable.

Interestingly there is now strong support for the idea that it is too little rest, rather than too much hard training, which is the cause of overtraining-like symptoms. Indeed British experts have recently suggested that we should talk about under-recovery, not overtraining – a subtle but significant difference. This will be discussed in more detail in Chapter 4.

Specificity

Put simply, what you train is what you improve. If you do lots of long slow running on flat surfaces, you primarily become good at running slowly for long distances on the flat. This might sound like another way of saying cross training (in other words, the use of other forms of exercise in a training pro-gramme designed to improve running perfor-mance) has no benefits, but this is not the case. There are other factors to be taken into account, such as:

- cross-over effects (for example, using cycling to increase leg strength for running uphill);
- training undertaken to combat individual weaknesses (for example, resistance exercises to improve ankle and pelvis stability); and
- the propensity for injury when the same activity is repeated many times (for exam-ple, other forms of aerobic training may be used to increase cardiovascular fitness while avoiding the stresses placed on ankles and knees while running).

This means that appropriate cross training can play a key part in a runner's overall train-ing programme. This is explored further in Chapter 3.

What it does however mean is that both the type of training (running, weights, cycling and so on) and how it is carried out (for example intensity and duration) will influence the resultant physiological training adaptations. It is important, therefore, to ensure that your training reflects the event for which you are training. Put another way, training is designed to cause positive adaptations to help your body cope with the stresses that will be placed on it in competition. This does not mean that the best way to prepare for a 2-day mountain marathon is simply to do lots of 2-day training runs. Instead, your training should include sessions designed to mimic the competition, for example long sessions (6 or 7hr) in the hills running 'in terrain' (in other words, on terrain similar to that on which you will be competing), carrying a rucksack and navigating.

Individuality

Everyone is different, and therefore to be effective training programmes need to be tailored to individual strengths and weaknesses. Even if two runners have similar times in a 6-mile fell race it does not mean that their training should be the same or that their underpinning physiology is the same. What would happen if they raced over longer or shorter distances? Would one be better than the other? Individual differences are numerous and include the following.

- Where you start from. In other words, your current level of fitness and training.
- What your potential limit is. We all have a genetic upper limit to how good we can be. This manifests itself in many different ways. The most obvious are visible ones such as height and physique (not body composition, as this can be changed, but the underlying bone structure). While off-road running is not as restrictive as say basketball or high jumping in terms of the

type of physique likely to excel, it is still advantageous to have quite a slim/normal build, rather than a tall, heavy one. Also of importance is your underlying physiology. While training can make a big difference, ultimately we all have genetic limits: what our maximum oxygen uptake can reach, our ability to tolerate and recycle lactate (lactic acid), our muscle fibre type and blood composition (these will be covered in Chapter 2). Overall, some scientists estimate that 70 to 80 per cent of endurance performance and ability to adapt to training is genetically determined.

- What you can handle. Not only are we different in our underlying physiology and genetics, but we also respond differently to training. For example, consider two runners who finish together in a 6-mile fell race. One might be very comfortable running 60 miles per week in training with three hard sessions. The other, however, might only be able to cope with 30 miles and two hard sessions without experiencing injury and illness problems.
- What your strengths and weaknesses are. Just because two runners finish a 6-mile race at the same time does not mean that either their physiology or other attributes critical to off-road running are the same. In fell running it is not uncommon for runners to be much better at either running uphill or descending, particularly where there is very rough ground underfoot.

There is therefore considerable truth in the statement that to be a good endurance runner you need to choose your parents carefully!

Reversibility

In the same way that our bodies adapt positively to training by becoming fitter, so they adapt to reduced, or no, training, by moving

Descending – a strength or a weakness?

back towards the level of fitness now required to maintain this new lifestyle. While it is possible to read 'horror' stories about runners losing all their hard-won fitness in a short period of time, such as 4 to 8 weeks, scientific research does not reveal quite such a depressing picture. Reducing or stopping training does lead to a decrease in fitness (with strength tending to be lost at a quicker rate than endurance). It is, however, certainly not the case that a few weeks lost due to illness, injury or work commitments will automatically mean a 'ruined' season.

Studies of older ex-athletes also suggest that these individuals do continue to benefit from their earlier training for a considerable time compared to their contemporaries who have been inactive all their life. However, they are usually not as fit as their colleagues who continue to exercise.

Hard/Easy

The best way to improve and get fitter is to mix harder training sessions with easy or recovery ones. This neatly combines two of the previous principles: overload and rest. In practice, this means varying what you do. For example, rather than running 6 miles steadily each day, giving a total of 42 miles per week, you are likely to see more improvement if you mix harder and longer runs, with shorter recovery runs as shown in the figure below.

One of the dangers of not having a training plan is that you may end up doing a lot of steady training and little hard or recovery training. As a result, your training will not be as effective as it could be for the same workload and the potential for incomplete recovery and boredom will be increased. Interestingly, another key factor thought to be significant in the prevention of staleness and overtraining (along with sufficient recovery) is ensuring that your training programme contains plenty of variety and does not become boring or monotonous. Most runners do not, however, go for total variety, preferring instead to have a few set runs which they do on a regular basis and can use to measure their progress.

The hard/easy principle is one that should not just be applied on a day-to-day basis, but also when planning your training on a larger scale: weekly, monthly, annually and, for some athletes, even longer than that. Many athletes who complete in Olympic events, for example, plan their training on a 4-year timescale. Use of the hard/easy principle, combined with progressive overload, leads to the periodization of training. This is the process by which the training year is broken down into smaller units of time, each with a slightly different emphasis and therefore with different training intensity and demand.

It is worth adding two more to these well-established training principles, to help with your planning.

	Monday	Tuesday	Wednesday	Thursday	Friday	Saturday	Sunday	Total
Example Training Week Mixing Hard and Easy Sessions								
unvaried	6 miles steady	6 miles steady	6 miles steady	6 miles steady	6 miles steady	6 miles steady	6 miles steady	42 miles
mixed	4 miles easy	7 miles including long efforts	8 miles steady	6 miles including some short strides	rest	7 miles including 3 miles sustained	10 miles	42 miles

Purpose

Fortunately (or unfortunately, depending on your point of view), it is not the case that the athlete who trains the hardest and the most will always be the best. Rather, it is those who train most appropriately for their event who will maximize their potential. As the saying goes, it is training smarter not harder that will bring about success.

Training with a purpose means ensuring that you know why you are doing a particular training session and therefore what benefits you hope to gain from it. Is it a recovery session? One to increase endurance? To improve your ability to run fast over rough ground? To practise navigation? Sometimes the purpose might be other than purely physiological. After a long day's work or travelling, going out for a short jog for recovery is for many people a good way of relaxing and soothing out any stiffness and tension.

Precision

When you set out to train you should not only aim to do so to the best of your ability, but to do so with precision. What does this mean in practice? Consider the following examples.

How often have you seen an athlete trying to lift large, heavy, weights who has succeeded only by distorting body position and movement pattern to bring in other muscle groups? The athlete may have lifted a greater weight, but did it have the desired training effect? Or might the bad technique lead to potential injury? The need for precision applies to all forms of training: doing technique drills, resistance exercises, stretching (how often is a perceived improvement in muscle length really down to a movement at a joint?), strengthening and core stability work.

Precision is also important in forms of training aimed towards improving cardiovascular fitness.

Consider the following example of runner

A and using the three p's: planning, purpose and precision. Planning tells us that runner A wants to do a training session to improve his ability to run at a sustained fast pace. Purpose suggests that the training session, after a warm-up jog, is a 20min sustained run on grass at a heart rate of 175bpm (beats per minute), which equates to runner A's lactate threshold. Precision means that, when on starting the effort, runner A finds that he can not run hard enough to get his heart rate over 175bpm, it indicates that he is too tired to get the desired benefit from the training session and should therefore stop and take it easy or rest instead.

Alternatively runner A might decide to do the training session with runner B, who is a better runner. When they set off together, in order to keep up with B, runner A's heart rate is soon up to 180bpm and then rises to 185. After 10min he is exhausted and has to stop. By running too hard and not being precise, runner A has failed to complete the planned session and therefore not benefited from its desired purpose.

For an explanation of lactate threshold (LT) and monitoring heart rate as an aid to training, *see* Chapter 2.

BUILDING YOUR CURRENT PROFILE

Once you understand the basic training principles, the next step is to consider what can be called your current training profile. As already noted everyone is different: we all have different physiological profiles, ability to tolerate different types of training, strengths and weaknesses, and these all need to be taken into account when designing a training programme. There are, however, a few other things, more related to personal circumstances, which must also be added to the equation. There is no point trying to follow a programme that calls for 7 hours' training per week if, realistically, you can only manage 5 hours'. Your personal training profile will provide you with the framework on which you can build a successful training programme that fits your personal requirements.

Where You Want to Be

You must identify your goal or target, which will most probably be a race or event, but which might be a more esoteric target, such as to reach a certain weight or to increase strength. It is worth making your target a measurable one, so that you will know when you have achieved it. Just aiming 'to become better at descending on rocky terrain' is quite vague. Instead, you could aim to improve your time over a particular descent either in training or during a race. Or if there is a fellow runner who is generally similar to you, but who always gets away from you on rocky descents, your goal could be to keep up with that person, as long as it does not adversely affect the rest of your race.

It is also important to make sure that your target is achievable. Setting goals that are either too easy or too hard can end up being demotivating and should be avoided. Ideally your goal should be achievable, but challenging.

Where You Are Now

Your starting point is your current training load, i.e. the training that you have been doing for the last 3 or 4 weeks. Depending upon your goal, your starting point might also include:

- other relevant skills (such as navigating);
- other related targets (for example if part of your goal is to lose weight or increase strength, then make sure that you make a note of your start level);
- any other requirements (such as equipment you will need but do not own or are not familiar with). If your goal is to compete in a mountain marathon, do you have

and know how to use a suitable tent and method of cooking? Trying to put up your tent for the first time in the pouring rain after being out all day in the hills is not a good idea.

Comfortable Training Load

Your comfortable training load is exactly what it says, the training load that you can comfortably handle both in terms of quality and quantity. It is the amount of training that:

- is hard enough to provide some training benefit;
- you can carry out without excessive physical or mental stress;
- does not require large sacrifices (for example time, social or family life) to achieve;
- does not cause your work or personal life to suffer;
- does not leave you excessively tired physically or mentally; and
- does not leave you vulnerable to colds and minor infections.

For most runners, their comfortable training load is usually the same as their current training load. Others, depending on the circumstances, might be doing less (for example through lack of motivation or when having a rest period) or more (for example in hard training or doing too much).

For most runners the comfortable training load forms the starting point for their training programme. With time, of course, the aim of training is to increase your comfortable load. As you get older, unfortunately, the converse tends to happen and your comfortable training load slowly decreases as your body takes longer to recover between hard training sessions.

Strengths and Weaknesses

All runners have their strengths and weaknesses. Most runners have a natural tendency

Make sure you know how to use your equipment before the event.

to train to their strengths because it is often 'easier' and more satisfying. Faster runners therefore do more speed work, those good at rough descents but who are slower runners spend a lot of time training over rough hilly terrain and less time doing sessions designed to improve basic speed. With off-road running, strengths and weaknesses do not just apply to the physiological aspects. For many of the disciplines, speed over different types of terrain, navigation, route choice, decision making and teamwork are all important.

Available Time

What time can you commit to your training without it adversely affecting your work, social or family life?

You may, for example, decide that you can happily commit 7 hours per week to training without it disrupting the other parts of your life or causing family friction. In order to have a 'hard' training week can you persuade your family that for one week in four for example you will be spending more time training, but that this will be followed by an easier week the next, and thus increased family time?

It is also important when thinking about your time commitment and planning your training to make sure you take into account other aspects of your life, for example plan easy training days or weeks to dovetail in with social or work commitments. Of course it is not just the actual training time that you need to think about it, but also the time

Are you more of an endurance or a speed-based runner? A simple way to think about this is to ask yourself if you stopped running for a couple of weeks which would you 'lose' or would suffer the most: your endurance or your speed? Would you find that after a fortnight that instead of being able to run for 15 miles you could only manage 10? Or that the distance covered during your 60sec repetitions has decreased significantly? Typically, what you lose the least is where your strength lies.

Another approach is to ask yourself which are you relatively better at:

- Running for long distances/time?
- Natural speed over shorter distances?
- Running at a sustained pace for 30 to 60min (i.e. threshold pace)?

You also need to consider your ability over different types of terrain. Consider your speed over:

- long gradual uphills;
- rough loose descents;
- short steep hills;
- fast undulating ground;
- fast descents;
- contouring;
- rough rocky ground;
- boggy heavy ground;
- thick forest; and
- open moorland.

Depending on the type of off-road competitions in which you plan to participate, you may have to race on all of these different types of ground.

spent travelling to and from training and chatting to others afterwards. These all eat into your available time.

BARRIERS AND TRAINING LIMITATIONS

Try to identify any barriers to training. If, for example you live in East Anglia, decent sized hills to train on are few and far between, so you will either have to travel at weekends or use alternative sources of training (in this case, cycling). Other barriers might be harder to overcome – many elite British orienteers base themselves in Scandinavia in order to train on suitable terrain.

You will also need to consider other limitations on your training. For example, you might have decided that you can commit 8 hours a week to training, but you can only fit in half-an-hour at lunch times during the week and need to make the rest up at the weekend.

Another factor to consider is your potential risk of injury, especially if you have an old injury or 'injury weakness'. This might mean

that while you have the time to train 8 hours each week, and overall your body can physically and psychologically cope with this amount of training, it cannot cope with this amount of pure running without a high risk of injury. In this case, alternative training methods such as cycling, running in the pool, weights, cross-country skiing and so on, will have to play a greater part in your training.

Likes and Dislikes

Finally, it is important to remember that off-road running, training and competing is meant to be enjoyable – this is why we do it. While it may be necessary, or advisable, to do some training sessions which you do not really enjoy (for many, this could mean flexibility and stability work), overall your training should be fun.

PUTTING TOGETHER YOUR PLAN

Daily Training

With knowledge of the basic training principles, plus your own personal training profile, you can now begin to build your own training programme. If you regularly read running magazines or books, you will be aware of the proliferation of suggested training programmes, each with a different emphasis and all promising faster times and better performances. Which is right? And how can you fit all the recommended 'key' sessions into a training programme? This is where knowing your strengths and weakness plus understanding the physiological effects of the different types of training will enable you to decide what is right for you. In other words, you will be able to plan.

While most people tend to work on a 7-day schedule for ease, others work to a 10-day or 2-week schedule in order to fit in all of the components they want to include. This is often the case for athletes who are following a multi-sport training programme.

There are, however, no set rules that work for everyone. Many runners find they perform and train better with only two effort sessions per week. On the other hand, there is also a view that occasional back-to-back hard sessions can give you an extra training boost if used carefully. There is also plenty of subjective evidence that as you get older you need longer to recover between hard sessions. The most important thing is what works for you. As a rule of thumb, however, you should aim to include:

- one long run every week or 10 days ('long' will vary according to the event for which you are training);
- at least one rest or very easy day each week

or 10 days plus a couple of other easier days;
- two, or possibly three, harder, speed or effort based sessions per week;
- additional stretching/resistance or core stability work.

Putting together a training programme will mean different things to different people. Some runners like to be very organized and structured, working out well in advance what they will do each week and each day and sticking to it. However, it is still vital to maintain a degree of flexibility. It is extremely common for a training programme to be disrupted by slight illnesses, injuries, family or work pressures or just by feeling 'off the boil' one day. It is, therefore, best to regard your plan as a guide rather than a rigid framework that has to be followed at all costs. Remember that the odd missed or altered training session is not as important as the long-term consistency of your training. Missing one training session is very unlikely to make a difference to your long-term goals, whereas completing a consistent period of training is.

Setting out a detailed training programme well in advance does not fit everyone. If you have a varied work or lifestyle pattern it may not be possible to predict from one week to the next what you will be doing and where. In these cases, detailed training programmes become, if not impossible, very difficult to follow. Trying to stick to a programme in such circumstances often becomes more stressful than the training itself. A more flexible approach will be necessary, but it must

Typical Weekly Structure for a Running Training Programme						
Sunday	Monday	Tuesday	Wednesday	Thursday	Friday	Saturday
long run	steady run	effort session	medium length run	possible effort session	rest or easy run	race, sustained, longer efforts or fartlek

Training With Others

Although some runners are very happy to train on their own, most enjoy and benefit from the company of others while training. The problem can be finding people of a similar standard, who also want to do the same training as you. Successful group training normally requires a degree of compromise, in other words flexibility within your training programme while still sticking to the overall plan. In terms of the actual training session to do, this compromise should not be too much of a problem. More problematic can be the speed that you train at, especially if you train with runners better than you. On the one hand, this may be an advantage because you are 'pulled' along and work hard. On the other hand, the danger is that you never get any easy recovery sessions as you are always working that bit harder. Alternatively, if you are the 'best' in a group, do you ever really push yourself hard? If you do tend to train with faster runners, then it is important to make sure that you very consciously have one or two easy/recovery days or runs a week. This might be by running on your own, or by going out with a different, slower, group than normal.

still enable you to ensure that you do the key training you need. Two possible options to consider are:

- Try to keep a couple of days/sessions sacrosanct. If you train with a group on a Tuesday evening, then wherever possible you should try to plan your work so that you will always be able to make that session. This, plus the two weekend days, would mean that you would be able to have three key sessions a week (which for most people is plenty), supported by whatever else you can fit in during the rest of the week (not forgetting some rest as well).
- Plan each week and the key sessions within it at the start of the week. For example you

might decide that while it is ideal to do two speed-based sessions a week, it is only realistic to expect to fit one in. You therefore want to make sure that, as a baseline, you do one long run, one interval-type session and one sustained run each week. At the beginning of each week, mentally plan how best to fit these three key sessions in around your work and family commitments. By doing this, your effort sessions will not always be on, say, a Tuesday, but could fall on any day of the week (although you should avoid scheduling the three key sessions on consecutive days). As long as you can achieve this, then you will be hitting your training targets. Hopefully, you may find that some weeks you are also able to find time for a third speed-based session, in which case this is a bonus.

Thinking in this way means that you are more in control, working to achieve your realistic baseline targets, rather than trying to fit in unrealistic, although desirable, targets all the time.

The Bigger Picture

Putting together a weekly training programme is one thing, but how do you progress it to make sure that it continues to provide you with the training stimulus that you need? Again, unfortunately, there are no hard and fast rules. Training really is about art using science. It is a case of finding out what works for you, fits into your lifestyle, and what your body can physically and mentally cope with.

When building a training programme it is important to take the following into account:

- Your plan should take you reasonably smoothly from where you are now to where you want to be, building up gradually. Some experts suggest that you should increase your weekly training load or

---

After Dark

Dark conditions and off-road running do not really go that well together. For many the winter months mean that off-road training is only practical at weekends. Sometimes, with a little ingenuity, things are not quite as bad as that and there are a few tips to think about before you resort to running only on roads or cross training in the gym.

- Is running at lunch time a possibility? Most cities and towns have quite a bit of green if you look for it. It is possible for example to be off-road within 5min of Leeds city centre and stay off for as long as you like (or your lunch time allows) by linking paths, parks, playing fields and the canal.

- Are there any stretches of grass lit by street-lights? While this may not be good for longer runs, it is often possible to find suitable areas to run repetitions on grass after dark, either on the edge of a park or round all-weather playing fields.
- Remember snow is a great light reflector. Snow on the ground will actually open up the running options after dark, assuming that you have suitable footwear.
- Have you thought about using either a head torch or orienteering night lamp? Especially on reasonably smooth surfaces, such as canal towpaths, a small head torch might make all the difference.

---

mileage by no more than 10 miles or 10 per cent of your current mileage per week.
- Be flexible. It is probable that illness, injury or work will disrupt your training at some time. If this happens, do not to try to go straight back to the point where you had originally planned to be in your build-up. At a minimum, you should start back where you left off, in other words start with the level of training that you were doing at the time of the interruption. Depending on how much you have lost, you may have to start further back than that, and then build back up to where you want to be.
- Aim for consistency. There is little point in having a really good, hard week's training if it means that you have to spend the next fortnight recovering.
- Take the rest of your life into account, as running and training are not the only stresses it will be under. Your body does not distinguish between different types of stress, whether it comes from training, travel, work, family or other sources. Your training programme should take this into account and not schedule hard weeks at times when you also have higher additional stresses elsewhere in your life. Take the

Christmas break for example: for some runners this is a time when, because they are not working, they aim to have a hard week's training. Others take it as a time to enjoy the festivities rather than train hard (see Chapter 4).

It is also important to think how you want to structure your training. Many athletes, runners included, use periodization. This involves breaking the training period (anything up to a year or more) down into manageable blocks of around 4 to 12 weeks each, each with a slightly different training focus.

Alternatively, you might prefer a gradual build up of distance and quality, using a basic weekly training pattern, with less emphasis on actual training blocks. In either case, do not aim for a straight line of increasing mileage and quality. Instead, think about working in steps. This might, for example, involve one week at your current comfortable training load, followed by a harder week (either increasing the mileage or the quality or both). The pattern is then repeated, with the mileage of the harder weeks slowly increasing. Over a 12-week period up to a race this might go something like:

Holidays

Many runners take running or activity-based holidays, either self-arranged or with one of the specialist tour operators. Alternatively, you might decide to use a block of your annual leave from work to get in some serious training at home. Great in theory, but with the potential for disaster if you get carried away on a burst of enthusiasm (yours and others) and try to embark on a very ambitious but unrealistic week or fortnight of training. The last thing you want to happen is for your training holiday to turn from a fitness boost into a cause of subsequent injury, illness or lingering over-tiredness. Not only will this put paid to your racing chances, you will also have wasted your holiday! To make the most of your break:

- plan (and have) an easy week's training on either side of your running holiday;
- give yourself time to recover from the travelling;
- make sure you increase the rest as well as the hard training (don't spend all your time sight-seeing if away or doing DIY at home);
- don't burn the candle at both ends;
- use the additional time to work on any strength, core stability or flexibility weaknesses;
- set a realistic target for the amount by which you actually increase your training.

Typical Annual Periodization of Training Programme

Oct	Nov–Jan	Feb–Mar	April–May	June	July–Sept
4 weeks active rest	12 weeks build up steady base mileage	8 weeks introduce strength work via hills and fartlek	8 weeks maintain mileage introduce speed work	4 weeks decrease mileage, taper, speedwork	12 weeks key racing period

miles per week: 30; 40; 30; 45; 35; 50; 35; 50; 40; 55; 40; 30

Other commonly used repeat patterns are:

- two weeks hard followed by one week easy; or
- two weeks comfortable training load, one week very hard, one week easy.

If planned correctly, you will end up doing the same, if not greater, volume of work compared to working to a straight-line increase. However, the hard weeks are harder and the easy ones are easier. Not only does this place a greater temporary training stimulus on the body, but more importantly also it gives more time to recover and therefore avoid burnout or overtraining.

Competing

The last part of the planning process is to consider competition. What must you do in the final phase of your preparation to ensure that you perform to your best? Not all competitions, however, are equal. Although competition may be your goal, it is also common for runners to use less important races as part of their training, both physically and mentally. This might involve using races over shorter distances as hard speed sessions, or racing over similar terrain and distance to improve 'race fitness'. While the former approach might be used for all races, the latter is more popular with those racing over shorter, rather than longer (i.e. 2hr plus), distances. Many runners and coaches feel that there is a need to race a certain number of

21

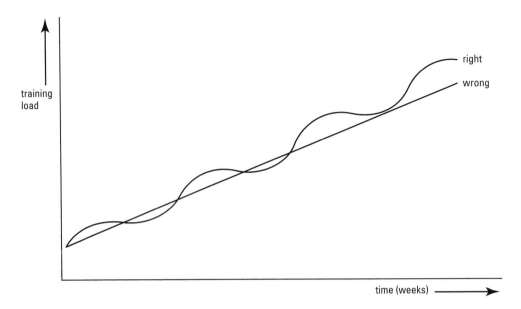

How to increase your training load.

times prior to a main competitive goal. Your best race will not be your first one, but maybe your third or fourth, once you are 'race fit'.

When using a race for training purposes, during the week beforehand most runners will either continue training as normal or ease off gently. If the race itself is not important, you might decide just to train through it, making no changes to your training leading up to or following the race and accept that you will probably be racing on heavy, tired legs. More usual is to ease down in the second half of the week before the race.

While the concept of tapering or easing down for a major competition is universally accepted, the best way in which to do so is not. Scientific studies on tapering have mainly been carried out with swimmers, although some have been done using runners and cyclists. Depending on the seriousness and severity of the competition, tapers of up to 4 weeks can be used. For most runners this is probably on the long side. Instead you should be looking to reduce the quantity of training you carry out in the final week or

couple of weeks, while maintaining some quality speed work (basically making sure your body does not forget how to run fast).

How much you taper is a personal choice. Some runners prefer to do virtually nothing in the final week (particularly for long, 2hr-plus events), while others only reduce their training a little. It is important to remember that running-based activities often require more recovery time than sports such as swimming or cycling where the body is non-weight bearing. While these sports require recovery time to enable refuelling and so on, they do not need time to recover from the pounding and subsequent muscle damage experienced when running. The forces going through the body on ground contact when running can be up to two to three times your body weight.

Experiment to find out what works best for you in terms of tapering for a race, and as a rule of thumb consider:

- using a stepwise approach, continuing to reduce the amount you do as you get nearer the event;

What is Race Fitness?

Depending on the event and the surface, 'race fitness' can mean one of a number of things:

- Being used to the specific race distance and intensity.
- Being mentally prepared for, and familiar with, the demands that will be placed on your body, for example the ability to be able to start fast and then hold a sustained pace.
- Having confidence gained from previous races that you can run hard for the distance.
- Having specific conditioning, for example the quadriceps muscles for fell races involving a lot of hard downhill running.
- Refining tactical awareness or getting your 'racing brain' in gear, for example in cross country races making sure that you are in the right place at the right time to cover any breaks.
- Knowing that you have got your pre-race routine and preparation sorted out and that you have checked out and tried any kit, equipment or shoes that you require.

Training Programme Easing Down Before a Race

	Sunday	Monday	Tuesday	Wednesday	Thursday	Friday	Saturday
normal training	long run	steady run	speed session	medium run	semi hard session	rest	sustained efforts
race week	long run	steady run	speed session	shorter run	steady/easy run with strides	rest	race

Not all runners like to take a rest day the day before a race, complaining that it makes them feel heavy legged and not 'smooth' when they start their pre-race warm up the following day. Instead they prefer to schedule a rest day 2 days before the race and then do an easy run plus some strides on the day before the race (in the example above, they switch the Thursday and Friday around).

- maintaining training intensity;
- reducing the amount you do per training session, rather than the number of training sessions (this helps keep the running action smooth). Some scientists suggest that you should reduce the number of training sessions by no more than 20 to 30 per cent.

There is no need to worry that reducing your training during the taper might lead to fitness losses. Scientific studies have shown that reductions in training of up to 60 per cent for 2 to 3 weeks do not cause reductions in $\dot{V}O_2$max or endurance performance.

When preparing for a competition, it is also important not to forget all the other things that are vital to ensure all goes as planned:

- **Nutrition:** in particular make sure that you fully restock your carbohydrate stores and that you are fully hydrated.
- **Rest:** remember to try not to spend too much time standing around or doing other energetic things instead of training.
- **Colds and bugs:** try and avoid them! Take extra care over your own personal hygiene. Try to avoid people with colds or other similar symptoms. If possible, reduce contact with children and avoid large crowds. Make sure that you wash your hands

regularly, in particular after touching frequently used surfaces such as telephones.

- **Clothing and footwear:** make sure that all clothing that you plan to race in or carry is comfortable and will not cause blisters or rubbing in the circumstances in which you plan to use it. For example, in most fell races you can guarantee you will be running on cambered slopes and you will be likely to have wet and muddy feet. Try out your footwear and socks in similar circumstances.
- **Equipment:** check and re-check it. If you know that the race you are planning to do requires the use of a compass, make sure yours works, does not have air bubbles in the face and that the housing glides smoothly. Trying to operate a stiff housing with cold, wet hands while also holding a map is not easy and best avoided.
- **Event timings:** work out how long you need between arriving at the event and the time you start. Some events can involve a long walk or jog from the car parking or registration point to the actual start. Add to that the time you need to prepare/warm up, add a final 15 to 20min in order to calculate the time when you need to arrive.

- **Event details:** make sure you know where the event starts, where the registration is, whether any areas are out of bounds or where you have to follow taped routes.
- **Event equipment:** many off-road events, fell races and mountain marathons have mandatory kit that you must carry with you for safety during the race.

Further aspects to do with competition preparation are covered in each of the chapters on different disciplines of off-road running.

TRAINING DIARY

The final aspect of planning your training is to write it down. You should ideally keep a note of what you plan to do, and you will most definitely need to record what you actually do; in other words, you need to consider keeping a training diary. Why? Keeping a diary will enable you to track your progress and to record what went right and what did not in your training. Over the months and years you should find that your training diary becomes an invaluable training aid, allowing you to monitor your progression, to record and check what did or did not work, and

Tapering							
Final weeks prior to a major competition as compared to the peak week's mileage:							
	Sunday	**Monday**	**Tuesday**	**Wednesday**	**Thursday**	**Friday**	**Saturday**
max training week, 60 miles	long run, 16 miles	steady run, 8 miles	speed session, total 8 miles	medium run, 10 miles	semi-hard session, total 8 miles	rest	sustained efforts/ shoter race total 10 miles
last 2 weeks, 45 miles	long run, 11 miles	steady run, 5 miles	speed session, total 7 miles	steady run, 8 miles	semi-hard session, total 6 miles	rest	sustained efforts, total 8 miles
30 miles	medium run, 8–10 miles	easy run, 4–5 miles	speed session, total 6 miles	rest	easy run with a few strides, total 5 miles	rest	race

therefore helping you to plan your training in the future. It is by using a training diary, for example, that you can easily look back and find:

- that brilliant taper that worked before your last big race;
- how long it took you to drive to a particular race last year;
- how much food you carried on your last mountain marathon – was it enough?
- what training you did the last time you were injured and how long it took you to recover;
- what times you did the last time you ran that particular training session;
- how much training you did for a particular race last year.

What is a training diary? At its most basic it is simply a record of the training you did that day, for example 'Monday, six miles'. However, just noting what you did is of limited use. Of more value is spending a little more time to record:

- the time and route you took;
- if doing efforts or speed work, what you did and how long each one took;
- how you felt;
- what your heart rate or perception of effort was;
- what the weather was like and who you ran with.

So, rather than just 'six miles' it becomes: 'Monday, six miles, 55 min. Adel wood loop with Julie. Weather good, wet underfoot, legs tired from yesterday.'

Some runners like to record more than this, writing detailed notes of each session, as well as including:

- hours slept;
- mood;
- weight;
- (for women) menstrual cycle phase;
- morning heart rate;
- weekly mileage or training volume;
- shoes used.

The training dairy then starts to become a tool to help you maximize training and avoid overtraining, which is covered in more detail in Chapter 4.

How you record this information is up to you. Many runners buy either a specialist 'running log' or an ordinary year diary with the right amount of room for what they want to write. Alternatively, you might decide to use one of the computer-based training logs or just an A4 file with either blank paper or specially designed sheets with spaces to record what you want in. If you chose to use a standard diary, it is worth reserving that diary just for your training, rather than using it for social and other information as well.

CHAPTER TWO
Physiology of Training

Or, what to put in your training programme. Before looking at the different types of training relevant to off-road running in Chapter 3, it is worth giving a brief overview of how the body works, as this will affect runners and their training.

This section is designed to provide runners with the background necessary to have a better understanding of the different types of training and the effects these have on the body. Those wanting more information should go to one of the recommended texts given at the end of Chapter 3.

MUSCLES

Muscles are soft tissues which are made up of numerous muscle fibres. There are three types of muscle, of which the one of most interest to us in this context is skeletal muscle. Skeletal muscles are attached, via tendons, at either end to bone. Movement occurs when muscles contract (get shorter) thus bringing their attachment ends (bones) closer together. In most cases, the movement occurs because one end of the muscle moves towards the other, rather than both moving at the same time.

Each muscle is made up of thousands of individual muscle fibres, which are grouped into bundles. If you look at lean meat, these groups of fibres can often be seen. Within each muscle fibre there are then thousands of smaller units, which contain two types of protein filaments (actin and myosin). While their names are not important in the context

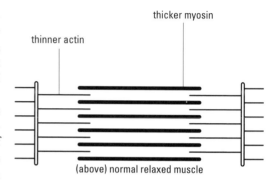

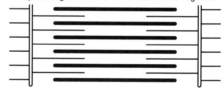

Arrangement of muscle filaments during rest and contraction.

of running, their actions are, as it is these which cause muscles to contact and therefore produce movement.

To enable this movement to happen, there are tiny cross bridges on the thick filaments which, by attaching and unattaching, pull the thin filaments closer (*see diagram above*). This action takes place simultaneously in all muscle fibres that receive the same nerve impulse.

Why, as a runner, is it important to know about this process? While the normal muscle action is one of shortening (called a concentric contraction), muscle can also contact isometrically. Here there is no change in muscle length; for example, when trying to push a building, you are using your muscles but not moving. Finally, there are also what are known as eccentric muscle actions, in which the muscle develops force as it is lengthening. The most obvious example for off-road runners is the quadriceps muscle used while running down hill; here it is contacting eccentrically to help control the descent.

The downside of eccentric muscle actions is that they usually result in 'tears', either in the cross bridges between the muscle fibre filaments, or in other components of the muscle cells, as the force placed on the muscle causes it to lengthen. This temporary, repairable muscle damage is thought to be the primary cause of delayed onset of muscle soreness, something that will be familiar to off-road runners who have been doing a large amount of downhill running. Typically, this manifests itself a couple of days afterwards with very sore quadriceps muscles that are stiff and painful to touch and in legs that have a tendency to buckle uncontrollably. Many people mistakenly put this delayed muscle soreness (which can also occur if you suddenly take part in some vigorous or unaccustomed exercise, for example if as a runner you play a one-off game of squash) down to a build up of lactic acid. It is not, it is due to these microtears and the subsequent repair process.

There is also more than one type of muscle fibre. Put simply, muscle fibres can be divided into two main types, 'fast twitch' and 'slow twitch'. While muscles will have a mixture of both types of fibre, the respective percentages of both are genetically determined and vary from person to person. Fast twitch muscles contract very quickly and powerfully but also tire quickly. Typically sprinters and other power-based athletes will have a greater percentage of this type of fibres. Slow twitch

fibres do not generate as much force, but can keep contracting for longer without becoming tired. Endurance-based athletes typically have a greater percentage of slow twitch fibres. Your make up of muscle fibre type is, in general, set by your early years and cannot be changed. However, there are some fibres which are in-between and it is thought that training can play a part in making these either more fast or slow twitch in characteristic. In practice, this means that as a runner your muscle fibre type will determine in which event you are most likely to succeed, and there is little you can do to change this underlying ability.

ENERGY SYSTEMS

Movement is caused by muscles contracting. This process, as do all others in the body, requires energy. The basic unit of energy used by the body for its actions is a chemical compound known as ATP (adenosine triphospate). The body's energy systems are the way in which sufficient ATP is produced to enable movement to occur and for it to happen within the required time frame. A 400m sprinter needs to cover that 400m in a much shorter time than the time in which a 10,000m runner needs to cover each 400m of a race, and therefore the sprinter needs to generate energy at a much faster rate. If ATP is the end product that can be used by muscles, the starting point is the food we eat. One of the aims of training is to make the body better at producing enough ATP for the actions we want it to carry out, in this case running.

Energy comes from carbohydrates, proteins and fats. Unless in extreme circumstances, most of the energy used during everyday life and when exercising comes from carbohydrates and fat, and only a small amount comes from protein. While even the thinnest runner has an abundant store of fat (enough energy to run over 1,000 marathons), the body's ability to store carbohydrate is limited (to around 90 to 120min of exercise at marathon running pace). This would not be a problem if fat could be used as an energy source as efficiently and as quickly as carbohydrate. Unfortunately, this is not the case. While a notional 1g of fat contains more energy (9kcal) than 1g of carbohydrate (4kcal) it also requires considerably more oxygen to be broken down to provide the same amount of ATP, and doing so therefore takes longer.

How then does the body make ATP from the food we eat, and in particular from fat and carbohydrate? The body has three ways of producing ATP which it uses depending on how quickly it needs to generate energy for example to move. These are known as:

- the ATP–PC system;
- the glycolytic or anaerobic system;
- the oxidative or aerobic system.

In each case the name describes how the system works. As a runner, by having a basic understanding of each, you should be better placed to understand the benefits of the different types of training you do.

ATP–PC System

The ATP–PC system is used when the body needs to generate large amounts of energy in a very short period of time, for example weightlifting or a 60m sprint. Muscle cells, as well as containing a little ATP, also contain a limited supply of a substance called phosphocreatine (PC) which can be used to make more ATP very quickly. This can occur without the need for oxygen. However, the body only has a very limited supply of ATP and PC, enough for around 3 to 6sec of all-out effort. The product creatine is an ergogenic (performance enhancing) aid which has been shown to increase the body's supply of phospocreatine and therefore its ability to

repeat short, all-out efforts.

For endurance-based athletes such as off-road runners, the ATP–PC energy system is probably the least important of the three energy systems, only coming into use in situations such as flat-out sprints at the end of races.

Glycolytic or Anaerobic System

The glycolytic or anaerobic system is the process by which the body is able to produce ATP without using oxygen. This is very important both when exercising at harder intensities and when a bout of exercise first begins and the aerobic systems take a little time to produce the amount of ATP required. Put simply, during the glycolytic or anaerobic energy system pathway (anaerobic means without oxygen), carbohydrate in the form of glycogen or glucose is broken down via a series of steps to a substance called pyruvic acid, in the process releasing ATP. In the absence of oxygen, pyruvic acid in turn is broken down to lactic acid. Muscles can only tolerate a certain level of lactic acid (also referred to as lactate) before further production is inhibited (to ensure the muscle does not become damaged) and the muscle's ability to contract is affected. This is usually felt as a severe burning sensation in the muscles, often combined with a feeling of 'tying up'. While many people regard lactic acid as a waste product, this is not actually the case. Once there is enough oxygen available (or the lactic acid has been transported elsewhere in the body where there is enough oxygen), it can be re-converted back to pyruvic acid and used as fuel.

As a runner you are probably familiar with the burning lactate feeling; for example, think how you feel if trying to run a flat-out 400m or for a couple of minutes. Training can, however, help you become better at dealing with lactic acid. First, you can become able to tolerate higher levels of lac-

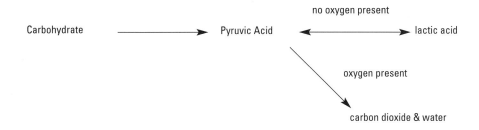

The breakdown of carbohydrate.

tate in the muscle before having to stop. Secondly, training can increase the intensity of effort (i.e. running speed) before lactate starts to build up. This is done partly by improving the body's ability to remove lactic acid from the working muscles and take it to other non-working muscles and the liver to be converted back to pyruvic acid. Typically you can produce enough energy this way for about 20 to 60sec of flat-out hard running.

Oxidative or Aerobic System

The oxidative or aerobic system is the process by which carbohydrates and fats (and to a lesser extent) proteins are broken down to form carbon dioxide, water and ATP. It needs oxygen to be present. Fat, although being the more energy-dense fuel (that is, it provides more energy or kcals per gram), needs more oxygen (and therefore time) to produce the same amount of ATP, compared to carbohydrate. In practice, this means that at low intensity levels fat provides a greater proportion of the required energy. As the intensity increases a greater proportion of carbohydrate is used. The body does not switch from one energy source to the other, rather it is always using a combination of sources, the proportions of which vary depending on the circumstances.

When carbohydrate is broken down aerobically, the process starts off the same as in the glycolytic pathway. However, when oxygen is present, rather than the pyruvic acid being converted to lactic acid it enters something known as the Krebs cycle, where in the presence of oxygen it is completely broken down to carbon dioxide and water, also generating ATP. Fats, or triglycerides, are first broken down into smaller units called fatty acids before also entering the Krebs cycle. This process takes place in the muscles in structures called mitochondria. It is to these that the oxygen is delivered and the foodstuffs are converted to ATP.

From an endurance runner's perspective, there are a number of ways in which training aims to affect the oxidative process in a positive manner:

- By increasing the body's efficiency at using fat as an energy source, therefore sparing the more limited carbohydrate stores. In practice you become able to use a greater percentage of fat as fuel at any given speed.
- By increasing the body's ability to provide oxygen to the muscles and therefore allowing them to continue to work aerobically rather than anaerobically.
- By increasing the number of mitochondria in the muscle cells and therefore the number of sources of aerobic energy production.
- By increasing the number of blood capillaries in the muscles, making it easier to deliver blood, and hence oxygen, to the muscle cells.
- By increasing general movement efficiency. This is the equivalent of getting more

29

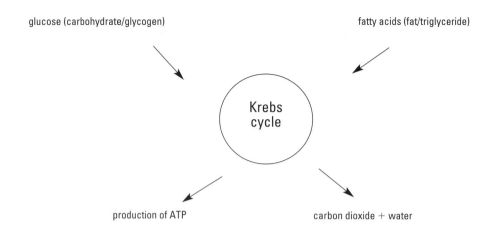

The Krebs cycle.

miles per gallon in a car (although this is not quite so handy if you are trying to loose weight!)

- By increasing the ability to provide the energy required through the oxidative system, therefore allowing you to run at a faster speed before lactic acid starts to build up.

As noted previously, it is not simply a case of moving from one energy system to another as you work harder and your running speed increases. Rather, a change in the amount of energy produced by a particular energy system takes place. This is perhaps best illustrated, and more importantly has most relevance to runners, by what is known as the lactate threshold (LT). The lactate threshold is also sometimes described as the lactate breakpoint or anaerobic threshold. These, however, are not one and the same thing, although there is still considerable scientific debate as to the exact relationship between them.

Even when exercising at low intensity levels, some lactic acid is produced in the exercising muscles. However, at low levels of intensity very little is produced. As you start to run faster, more lactic acid is produced by the muscle; however this is matched by the body's ability to transport the lactic acid to other sites (such as the liver, heart, other well-oxidated muscles) and be 'recycled'. This shows itself as a low level of circulating lactate in the blood, but no feelings of real discomfort and with a steady breathing rate. At this point, the muscles are still mainly obtaining their energy from aerobic energy sources.

As you begin to run faster, more lactic acid is produced, but up to a certain point (the LT) this is matched by the body's ability to remove the lactic acid from the exercising muscle. If you were to measure the level of lactate in the blood at this point, you would find no more than a slight increase.

As the speed increases further, you reach a point at which the amount of lactate circulating in the blood rises (partly reflecting an increased use of the anaerobic energy system and partly a reduced rate of lactate removal from the working muscle). The point or speed at which this increase occurs is the LT. At speeds below this it is possible to run for a considerable length of time; above it and you will soon start to breathe more heavily (in order to remove carbon dioxide) and tire. LT equates to approximately the sustained speed that you can run at for around 1 hour, that is, somewhere around 10km or 10 mile race speed for most runners.

The LT is therefore a critical point for endurance runners. The higher the LT, the faster the speed at which you can run without an excessive build up of lactic acid. Some scientists feel that a person's LT is the most important predictor of endurance performance for events from 5,000m to marathon distance. Appropriate training sessions to improve this value are therefore crucial.

CARDIOVASCULAR SYSTEM

The cardiovascular system (CV) consists of the heart, lungs, blood vessels and blood. It is basically the body's transport system. It is used to transport oxygen from the lungs to the working muscles (and to take away carbon dioxide, water and other products). It is also essential for keeping the body at the right temperature, transporting food from the gut to the muscles and for storage, ensuring that the brain has enough energy and for carrying nutrients to help repair damaged tissues. In fact, the CV system reaches every cell in the body.

The primary importance of the CV system in an endurance-running context is in its ability to transport oxygen from the lungs to the working muscles. The maximum oxygen uptake ($\dot{V}O_2$max) is the maximum amount of oxygen you are able to get from your lungs to the working muscles and use for energy processes. It is usually expressed as ml per kg body weight per minute or ml/kg/min. Along with the lactate threshold (LT), $\dot{V}O_2$max is felt to be a key determinant of endurance capacity. Unfortunately however, unlike LT, it is estimated that around 80 per cent of a person's $\dot{V}O_2$max is genetically determined. You can only improve your $\dot{V}O_2$max by around 20 per cent with training. (There is currently considerable debate within the scientific community around the whole area of $\dot{V}O_2$max, the terminology used, and what is actually measured. This, however, does not detract from its importance as a concept and its value to endurance athletes.)

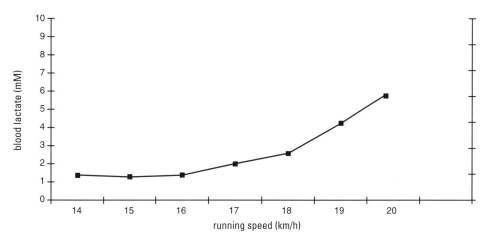

The relationship between running speed and blood lactate. (Taken from physiological support to UK athletics: protocols procedures and data interpretation by Dr Andrew Jones.)

Lungs

The lungs are where oxygen enters into the bloodstream and carbon dioxide is expelled into the atmosphere. The movement of air into and out of the lungs is known as ventilation. In healthy (non-smoking) individuals, this part of the CV system is not felt to be a major limiting factor to getting enough oxygen to the working muscles, even during maximal exercise.

Blood

Oxygen is carried to where it is needed in the body by the blood. Oxygen is not carried 'loose' in the blood, rather it is bound to red blood cells via a carrier called haemoglobin. The greater the concentration of red blood cells and haemoglobin in the blood, the more oxygen you can get to the working muscles. Men typically have higher haemoglobin values compared to women (14g/ml blood compared to 12g/ml). Haemoglobin is an iron-based compound and it is important to ensure that you have an optimal iron intake in your diet. This is particularly so for vegetarians, who tend to eat less iron, and women, who tend to have lower energy, and therefore iron, intakes and greater iron losses via menstruation.

Altitude training, blood doping and the use of EPO (erythropoietin) all aim to increase the number of red blood cells. However, the latter two are both classified as doping methods and therefore banned. The danger of this, particularly where EPO is concerned, is that increasing the number of red blood cells also increases the thickness of the blood. This means it is more sluggish and difficult to pump round the body (think of the difference between thick oil and water) and is thought to have been directly related to the deaths of some users.

One effect that endurance training has on the blood is to increase its volume, which in turn can mean a slight decrease in the concentration of haemoglobin present, but not the overall amount. This is sometimes referred to as 'athletic anaemia'. Where the blood goes around the body depends on what it is doing. At rest, some 20 to 25 per cent goes to the stomach and intestine, with just 15 to 20 per cent to the muscles. During heavy exercise, around 80 to 85 per cent goes to the muscles and just 3 to 5 per cent to the gut. One of the reasons thought to be linked to stomach ache or problems experienced if you run too soon after eating is that there is still food waiting to be digested in the stomach, but not enough blood to enable the process to be completed.

Veins, Arteries and Capillaries

The veins, arteries and capillaries carry the blood around the body. Capillaries are very fine vessels, sometimes no more than one red blood cell thick, that supply blood directly to the muscle fibres. One of the benefits of endurance training is that it increases the capillary density in muscle (that is, it increases the number of capillaries) and therefore increases the body's ability to deliver oxygen to that muscle. More oxygen means that the body is able to work harder aerobically, rather than anaerobically which would lead to a build up of lactic acid. In turn, this means that the rate of production of lactic acid is more likely to be matched by the rate of removal.

Heart

The heart is the body's pump, which keeps the blood moving around the body. It is a muscle and like other muscles adapts with training, becoming bigger, stronger and more efficient. Unlike skeletal muscle the heart, which is cardiac muscle, is not under conscious control, and therefore we cannot directly control its contractions. Your heart rate is the rate at which the heart beats, usually expressed as beats per minute. This, plus the amount of blood the heart is able to pump out at each contraction, influences how much blood and therefore how much oxygen reaches the muscles. Everybody has a minimum (or resting) and a maximum heart rate. The maximum value is largely determined genetically and tends to fall with age. The resting value, while having a genetic component, is also influenced by fitness. The fitter you are, the lower your resting heart rate is likely to be. Resting or morning heart rate can be used to help monitor whether you have fully recovered from the previous day's training (*see* Chapter 3).

From a training perspective, heart rate can be an important tool. It is easily measured, either using a heart rate monitor or by taking your pulse at the radial (wrist) or carotid (neck) points, and it directly reflects the amount of work being done during whole body, endurance activity. Broadly speaking the faster you run, the higher your heart rate will be. This relationship is a linear one until the very end, when the increase tends to level out (*see* diagram below). What this means in practice is that it is possible to monitor your training by measuring heart rate. With a little bit of more-detailed knowledge about heart rates and in particular your own individual values this can become a useful aid to help ensure that your training is doing what you want it to do. This will be covered further in Chapter 3.

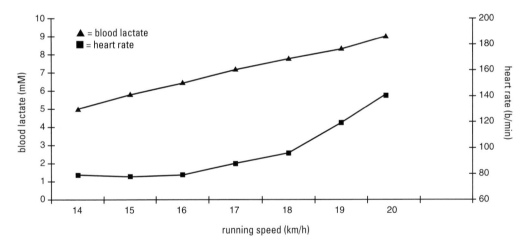

The relationship between running speed, blood lactate and heart rate. (Taken from physiological support to UK athletics: protocols procedures and data interpretation by Dr Andrew Jones.)

CHAPTER THREE
Types of Training

Training is about improving your performance, but what type of training? This section will look at the different types of training and consider how they can help running performance, in other words, how they can influence the way in which the body works by causing positive adaptations in the body's physiology. The principles and types of training covered, while discussed in running terms, can also be applied to other forms of endurance training, such as swimming and cycling.

When thinking about training, and reading about the different types of training given, it is very important that you keep in mind a very clear idea of what you are aiming for. The disciplines covered by this book range from short races (20min or so) to relatively long events (2 days for mountain marathons), so it is important to apply the principles to the event. The chapters on the individual off-road running disciplines also include sections on training where the specifics for each event are considered in more detail.

Finally, as you start to build your own training programme, remember that you need to maintain your strengths as well as work on your weaknesses. Failing to do either of these will mean your performances will not be as good as they could be.

STEADY OR CONTINUOUS RUNNING

While at a first glance the term steady running and what it means seems quite simple – running steadily – things can become a little trickier if you ask 'what is steady?' or 'what does steady mean?' Dr Andy Jones, one of Britain's top endurance physiologists, often divides runners into two types: those who have a tendency to do their steady runs quite hard (with no talking), and those who take them very steadily. The potential downside for the former is being left too tired to get full benefit from their designated hard sessions. For the latter, the downside is not running hard enough to benefit fully from the training, but with the advantage of being able to do loads of talking.

It is important therefore to find a balance to your steady running. Theoretically this can be done by heart rate, but just as important is to work 'by feel' and by learning to know your body, making sure that you do not push too hard at the wrong time. In practice there are two slight difficulties with using heart rate.

First, a quick glance at the various published tables giving suggested percentages of maximum heart rate that correspond to set training intensities shows there is no unanimous approach. Some suggest three training zones (or heart rate intensities), others five, each with slightly different percentages. Some figures give considerable flexibility, giving a 20 to 30 beat range. And this is without taking into account your own individual make up and training status. For example it is not uncommon to find that well-trained endurance runners as a result of increasing their lactate threshold (see Chapter 2) are able to run steadily at 80 to 85 per cent of their maximum heart rate, rather more than the normally recommended 60 to 70–75 per cent.

If you want to use heart rate to control your training to this degree, it is well worth paying to undertake a physiological test, as this is the only way to ensure that the values you use are right for you. This will be discussed further later.

Secondly, when running off-road, and particularly in extreme terrain (off the civilized path), the nature of the ground you will be trying to run over, plus the need at times to negotiate obstacles such as fences, stiles, bog, streams and rocky areas means that it will be very difficult to use heart rate to monitor your training. In these circumstances, obtaining a steady reading rather than one which is continually going up and down is near impossible. Here, it is best to go by feel.

For some of the longer events and those in more extreme terrain and topology, steady running should perhaps read steady training, as there are bound to be periods of walking involved due to the steepness, distance or surface underfoot.

Many people separate steady running from easy running. Easy running may or may not, in turn, be the same pace as that used to warm up and down prior to hard sessions. The difference is pretty much one of semantics, with easy running being at the slow end of steady. Whether you set yourself a formal difference is up to you. However, it is worth

Typical mixture of walking and running in a fell race.

making sure that you consciously have one or two day's training that really are easy days every week to 10 days.

Sometimes, particularly with steady running, the acronym KISS seems most appropriate: keep it simple stupid.

LONG RUNS

Long runs are really steady runs, just long ones. They can be anything in length from 60 to 90min (for races of similar or shorter length) to 6 to 7hr or longer in preparation for a mountain marathon. The latter is on the extreme side (but often necessary) for those events. For most runners their long run is normally 90min to 3hr depending on their race target.

While coaches, scientists and experts accept the need for long runs, views differ on the question of how hard they should be. Some suggest that it is time on your feet which is important and that the run can or should be done at an easy or steady pace, thus optimizing the aerobic fuel delivery system, including the body's ability to use fat as an energy source, as well as getting the body used to carrying out the running action for that length of time. Others champion the need to do long runs at a reasonably fast pace. Therefore for those competing over similar distances the pace is only slightly below race pace. This of course makes for a hard-feeling run, meaning you will be more tired the following day. On the other hand, in terms of specificity, the session is closer to the conditions of the event for which you are training.

Which is right? Well, both ways can work. If you look at the training carried out by top distance runners (albeit road runners), then for every one who ran 'slowly' on their long runs (Steve Moneghetti, Ingrid Kristiansen), there are others who ran 'hard' (Grete Waitz, Steve Jones). Whichever you decide on,

remember to balance its effects with the rest of your training. In particular, if you go for the faster approach your long run becomes a hard session which needs to be balanced with some easier recovery ones. Similarly, if you have raced the day before, then it is sensible to take it more steadily.

SUSTAINED OR THRESHOLD RUNS

Other common terminology for this type of training is tempo, fast, hard or race (10km – 10 mile) pace. There is good evidence that sustained running at a pace around your LT is an excellent way of helping to either 'push' the threshold upwards (by doing sustained runs of 20 to 45min at just below threshold pace/heart rate) or to 'pull' it up (doing repetitions of 1km to 2 miles with short recoveries). Improving your LT means that you are able to run at a faster pace before you start to experience a build up of lactic acid in the muscles.

There is obviously quite a difference between a sustained run of 20min compared to a 45min run (although in fact the physiological difference is not as great as first might be thought). The length of your sustained runs will depend on what you are preparing for: if your aim is an 8km cross country race, then sustained runs of 20 to 25min make sense; alternatively, for long trail or fell races upwards to an hour are needed. The important thing is to set off at a fast speed, but one that you feel that you can maintain for the whole length of the run, the aim being to run at a fast but constant pace the whole way. If you are using a heart rate monitor this should show a fairly constant heart rate the whole time, although it is likely to drift slowly upwards over the course of the run. This phenomenon is known as cardiovascular drift and is explained by the fact that the amount of blood pumped out of the heart with each beat (the stroke volume) falls slightly with time, particularly in the heat. Therefore, in order to maintain the same amount of blood (cardiac output) circulating in the body, heart rate must rise (cardiac output = stroke volume × heart rate). If you know your LT heart rate zone, then you need to make sure that you stay within this when doing sustained runs.

You may find that setting out to run at a sustained pace for over 20min is daunting – after all it will be a hard session and while it might not hurt there will be some discomfort. If so, an alternative is to split the session into shorter blocks, with short recoveries in-between, and to aim to run at the same speed/heart rate for each one. Rather than a sustained 40min run you might therefore do:

- 4 × 10min, with 1min recovery between each;
- 3 × 12–15min, 2 to 3min recovery;
- 2 × 20min, 2 to 4min recovery.

It is also possible to do this type of session running uphill. This will not only help improve your LT, but also condition your leg muscles for long sustained climbs, which is very important in particular for mountain and fell racing. The only downside is that you normally get a much longer recovery running back downhill to the start of each effort. If you have a long enough hill, for instance in the Alps or Kenya, this is not a problem as you can do the session in one go. This down-hill period should be used to help with your downhill conditioning (this is not needed so much for mountain racing, where most races are uphill only) by using a quick turn round and brisk descent.

Another session which can be used to provide a below threshold heart rate is 20:20 or 15:15; that is, running hard for 20sec and then coasting or running steadily for 20sec. This pattern is repeated for 10 to 20min. The easiest way to do this is to use the repeat countdown facility on a wristwatch.

Alternatively, you could work out how many steps you take in 20sec and count them out each time. A 20:20 pattern is often easier to co-ordinate, particularly if the countdown feature on your watch beeps for 10sec at each changeover point.

If this is done as a hard session then not only will you have carried out a series of accelerations and semi-sprints, but your heart rate during the session should have been at a level to be of positive benefit to your LT. The faster bursts of running help in another way too, helping your body adjust to running fast from a proprioceptive perspective. In this respect, it is a good session to use after a lay-off due to injury or end of season break as a way of re-introducing your body to faster, harder running.

This type of session also adjusts easily to being a semi-hard one, where the fast sections are run at a pace that is 'fast relaxed' rather than 'fast pushing it'. This makes a useful second or third fairly hard session of the week, or one to do a couple of days before a race.

FARTLEK

Fartlek is a Swedish word, meaning speed play, and it is as the name suggests, playing with speed. Classically, fartlek involves alternating bouts of running (or walking) at different speeds with little structure, going instead on how you feel. If you are with a group, you might each take turns to select when the next effort starts and how long it is. The efforts, normally varying from 30sec to 5min in length, can be determined either by time or by landmarks. Many running clubs will have set winter fartlek routes, which are never written down but everyone learns, containing a series of efforts of different lengths, the start and finish of which are identified by roads, lamp-posts, and so on. If using time alone, the addition of a mixed off-road terrain route will ensure that you get used to running hard over the 'difficult' bits.

Normally a fartlek session will total some 15 to 30min worth of efforts, with a warm up and warm down. Fartlek sessions tend to be less pressured or threatening than more structured interval based ones; yet they can result in just as much hard work. Here, however, you have to be honest with yourself as the less structured approach means it is also possible to 'get away' with doing less.

EFFORTS OR INTERVALS

This is basically running fast: either faster than your predicted race speed, or the same speed but for shorter distances. The potential content of an interval session is limitless (or limited only by the imagination of the session setter). Much of what you read would lead you to believe that there is some mystical formula to setting just the right session for the effect you want to obtain on that day. In practice, it is more about achieving consistent periods of hard work following broad principles (and including enough variety to prevent boredom).

The basics of interval sessions are running a number of repetitions, either judged by distance or time (or both), with a set recovery between each (time/distance determined). While many runners associate this type of training with running on a track, equally effective sessions can be achieved on good grass or dirt surfaces (which have the advantage of being more compatible to the racing surface) or roads (preferably well lit, not busy ones, such as roads on housing or industrial estates in the evening). There are plenty of elite off-road runners who never train on a track, preferring instead to use other surfaces. These tend to provide a less threatening and pressured environment.

Running on the track can also leave you with sore legs and Achilles tendons, especially if wearing spikes. Other runners prefer the discipline of the track and the fact that you know exactly how well or badly you are running: once around is always 400m! If you have never run on a track and want to do so, then be prepared to take a couple of sessions to adapt and to feel that you are running smoothly. This might seem a bit strange given that the track is flat and smooth, but you need time to adapt to any surface, even this one.

What then to do in your intervals? This depends on what benefit you want to get from them, in particular in terms of what energy systems you want to stress and what speeds and distances you want your body to become accustomed to.

Sprinters and middle-distance runners will frequently do sessions consisting of a few fast repetitions with long recoveries between

Typical Interval Sessions Used by Different Types of Runners		
	Interval session	Recovery
400m runner	2 × 3 × 300m	3min between each 300m, 10min between sets
5,000m runner	4 × 5 × 300m	20sec between each 300m, 2min between sets
10,000m runner	12 × 400m	slow 200m jog between each
marathon runner	20–30 × 400m	100m jog between each

reps = repetitions, the number of interval runs carried out
sets = groups of repetitions
i.e. 2 × 3 × 300 = 2 sets of 3 reps of 300m each, with 3min recovery between each rep, and 10min between each set

each. Endurance-based runners, on the other hand, will do sessions covering much greater distance, with shorter recoveries between each effort, even if the actual length of the effort is the same.

Typically, the longer the efforts and the shorter the recovery, the more the session is geared towards aerobic endurance improvements compared to anaerobic, speed-based goals.

When putting together an interval-based session the following variables need to be considered and set; and with time, changed to ensure continued progression (always, of course, bearing in mind the purpose of the session):

- length of the efforts (in time or distance);
- number of efforts (in one set or multiple sets);
- recovery between efforts (in time or distance or both), also between sets if used;
- speed of the efforts.

When setting interval-type sessions some athletes and coaches prefer variety, rarely doing exactly the same session twice, some prefer consistency, repeating two or three sessions on a weekly basis, while others have one or two key sessions that they use every 4 to 6 weeks to gauge progress. There are advantages and disadvantages of each: for example, do you like to compare your training on a week-to-week basis, accepting that it will not always be a smooth upwards curve? As always, it is important for you to identify the approach which is best for you.

One point to note about interval training relates to heart rate. When you start running your heart rate rises steadily, it does not just jump up to a particular value. Using heart rates as an indicator of work for short (less than 60 to 90sec) work is therefore of limited value as your heart rate is unlikely to have settled by the time you end the effort.

HILLS

Most off-road running involves hills; yes there are some trail races which may follow a canal bank, but generally speaking off-road running means you are going to come across hills, both up and down, and therefore you will need to train for both.

Uphill

Taking aside the fact that you will probably be racing on hilly terrain, hills can be a useful component of any middle/long distance runner's training. They can be used to help improve style or technique, leg drive and strength, and overall body strength as well as

---

Examples of Typical Endurance-Based Interval Training Sessions

Distance-Based Session	Time-Based Session
12 × 400m, 100–200m jog recovery	12 × 70–90sec, 45–90sec recovery
6 × 800m, 200–400m jog	6 × 2½–3min, 2min jog
6–10 × 1,000m, 200–400m jog	6–10 × 3–4min, 2min jog
5 × 600; 400; 200; 200m jog between each effort	5 × 90sec; 60sec; 30sec, 30sec jog between each
200; 400; 600; 800; 1,000; 800; 600; 400; 200; 200m jog between each	45; 90; 120; 180; 240; 180; 120; 90; 45sec; 60sec jog between each

The above are typical examples; however, these need to be taken in context rather than on their own.

cardiovascular fitness. How you use hills in training will vary, depending on your race targets and your own personal profile.

- **Short hills** (30 to 60sec) can be used to work on running action and style. This is done by concentrating on maintaining a good running action and leg drive; while the session should be a hard one, technique is more important than time. Alternatively, you can attack shorter hills, really working on powering your way up them. This will help in terms of increasing leg strength as well as improving the ability to apply sudden bursts of speed in races.
- **Medium hills** (2 to 5min) provide a good stimulus for improvements in aerobic capacity as well as specific hill-climbing musculature. Those who regularly run on the hills tend to have much more well-defined quadriceps (front thigh) muscles as compared to road runners. With both short and medium hills it is worth including sessions where you do not stop at the top of the hill. Rather, you carry your effort on over the hill for another 10 to 15sec to get used to running over hills, as you will have to do in races.
- **Rolling hills:** many runners deliberately include steady or fartlek runs over hilly courses, thus getting used to the ever-changing stride patterns and subtle technique changes that occur.
- **Long hills** (5min plus) can be used by those who plan to race over such distances. For example, European mountain races

Hill training.

may involve running uphill for anything from 30min to over 2hr. They are also beneficial to runners who will be racing on flatter terrain: Kenyan distance runners are renowned for including long (90min) uphill runs in their training. The key here is to ensure that you control the pace and do not set off too fast; these sessions should be about uphill conditioning, with heart rates at the top of steady, lower threshold pace.

Downhill

Being able to run downhill, or descend, is an art and for most off-road runners is a very important skill. Being able to descend well means that not only can you take time out of those who can not, but also that you can do so at a time when you are 'coasting' and recovering for the next flat or uphill bit. Good descenders give the impression of falling effortlessly downhill at speed, be it a grassy bank, a steep rocky path, or a scree slope. Others make more of a meal of it, at times appearing to nearly 'refuse' and stop at the top, but certainly slowing down.

In practising descending it is important to work out what is the best technique for you, and what technique is best for different types of terrain.

- Some runners lean slightly back, others say you should do the opposite, therefore encouraging a sort of free-fall action. Typically, shallow descents are best with a slight forward lean and steeper ones leaning back into the hill.
- To accompany your stance, use your arms. Classic fell descending technique sees runners windmilling with their arms to aid balance.
- Make sure you look ahead and try to pick out a decent line at least a couple of paces ahead.
- Be prepared for an unstable, slippery or

slanted platform for your foot.
- Try not to stay on your foot too long, think light and fast, aiming to skim over the ground and not brake. Use your feet to touch the ground and off again, to maintain speed not to reduce it. Not only will heavy braking slow you down and cause you to lose momentum, it will also result in more eccentric muscle damage and therefore subsequent soreness.
- Work out which footplant works best for you in different circumstances: heel? toe? flat foot? Many runners go for just the toes on a shallow hill, bringing the whole foot into play in steeper, rougher stuff (this will maximize the use of the studs if wearing fell shoes).
- Above all, practise; not only will this give you specific muscle conditioning, but also confidence, vital for fast descending.

FLEXIBILITY

Much is written about the need for flexibility, and certainly if you have restricted flexibility, particularly in the pelvis/lower-limb area, your running is likely to be adversely affected. There is, however, little evidence linking better flexibility and doing lots of stretching with improved endurance performance. What is important is achieving and maintaining the level of flexibility appropriate for your needs. It is probably fair to say that middle distance runners and sprinters require a better level of flexibility, while many international endurance runners are notoriously poor in this area.

If you think you need to work on this area but are unsure about the best way to either improve or maintain your flexibility, you should seek the advice of a chartered physiotherapist. For most off-road runners the most important factor is what could be called dynamic stability; in other words, how the muscles and joints cope with the ever changing terrain underfoot without damage.

STRENGTH

For many runners it is enough just to run. However, a limited amount (one or two sessions a week) of strength work would probably be beneficial, particularly if you have a sedentary job. In addition to the obvious benefits, for example ensuring that your abdominal and back muscles are strong enough to hold your pelvis in place (thus helping prevent sciatica-type problems), the participation in many off-road running events will benefit from a degree of upper body strength. For example:

● mountain marathons require you to run while carrying a rucksack for 2 days;
● most fell races involve bouts of hard uphill walking where you are using your arms to push off from your legs, and some require a degree of scrambling.

In many ways the easiest and best type of strength training for runners is circuit training. As well as requiring limited equipment, the movements involved tend to be more dynamic ones and therefore more akin to those used running and racing. A typical circuit might consist of twelve exercises, mixing arm, lower body and trunk exercises, with 45sec of effort on each exercise before moving on to the next (no rest). The circuit is then repeated two to four times. Exercises can be changed on a weekly basis to prevent boredom and cover a wider range of muscle groups.

Other alternatives would be to use free or fixed (multi-gym) weights. Both these will require greater attention to technique, particularly with free weights. For other circuit training ideas, *see* Rex Hazeldine, *Fitness for Sport* (The Crowood Press, 2000).

STABILITY

Over the last couple of years athletes and coaches have become more aware of the importance of stability training.

What is stability? Typically people tend to use the term 'core stability' when referring to the lower back or pelvis. This is, however, a limited view and taking a wider perspective is preferable. Here, core stability refers to the stability and functioning of the major body platforms: shoulder (or scapula), pelvis, knee and ankle.

For off-road runners the pelvis and ankle are probably the two most important platforms, for others, such as javelin throwers and swimmers for example, the shoulder is more important.

Instability or 'an excessive range of movement for which there is no protective muscular control' means that the likelihood of problems is greater. In the case of the pelvis, while acute problems may occur, these are more likely to manifest themselves as chronic pain either in the lower back/groin area or down the legs (an apparent feeling of a pulled hamstring plus the inability to use the leg properly is a common symptom). Ankles, on the other hand, are more susceptible to acute problems, something exacerbated by the nature of the terrain underfoot which tends to be challenging to say the least.

What therefore you are looking for in terms of stability is 'the ability to control the whole range of motion of the joint' (Norris, 2000), particularly as it is functionally relevant to the typical movements demanded by your sport.

It is beyond the scope of this book even to attempt to describe appropriate exercises and training regimes to improve ankle or pelvis stability. While there are a number of specialist texts as well as articles in running magazines on this topic, probably more than with any other type of training, the word 'precision' is critical to effective stability training. Stability training involves carrying out a series of exercises using either body weight or equipment such as rubber tubing, Sissel cush-

Example Circuit Training Session

Full sit ups

Press ups

Squat thrusts

Back raises

Example Circuit Training Session *continued*

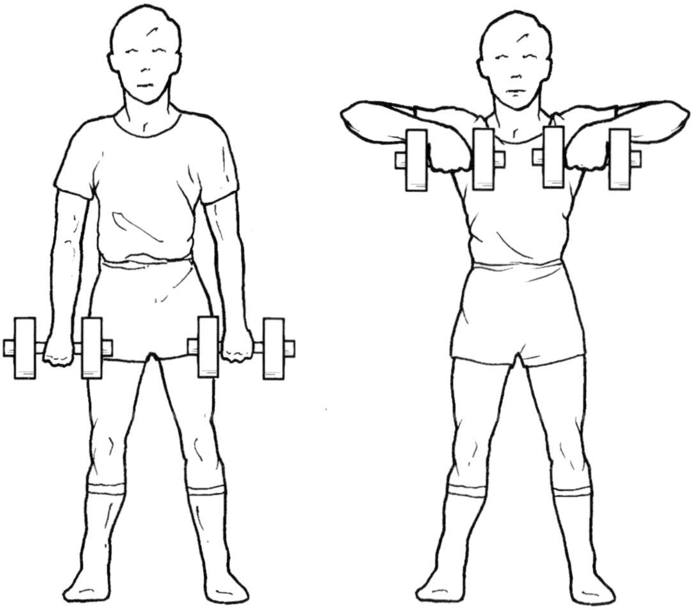

Upright rowing

Step ups

Half sit ups with twist

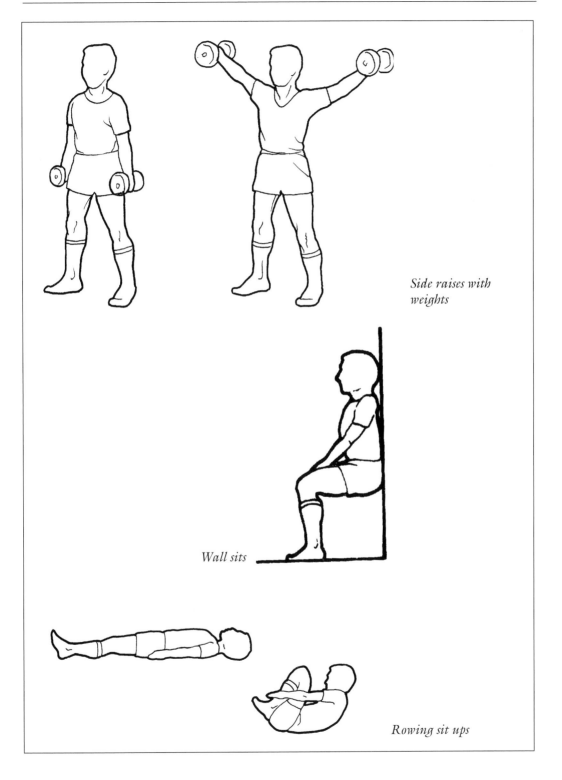

Side raises with weights

Wall sits

Rowing sit ups

Example Circuit Training Session *continued*

Dumb-bell curls

Burpees

ions or Swiss balls to help strengthen the stabilizer muscles. Rather than being directly responsible for muscular action, they work to maintain correct joint positioning at all times. It is therefore critical to ensure that when carrying out the exercises that your body alignment is correct. Otherwise you may spend hours doing exercises that subsequently prove to be ineffective because your body was incorrectly positioned while doing them. For this reason working with a specialist (such as a chartered physiotherapist) is recommended. It should only take a couple of sessions for the physiotherapist to assess you and ensure that you are carrying out the exercises correctly.

Having said that, for those with a disposition for weak ankles, or just generally, time spent on a wobble board or Sissel cushion to strengthen the ankles will not be wasted.

CROSS TRAINING

The principles of training imply that the best way to train for off-road running is to run off-road. Although broadly speaking this is true, cross training can however play a very effective part in any training programme:

● as a way of training when you are injured and can not run, or when the amount of running you can do is limited by the likelihood of injury;
● supplementary training to either overcome a weakness (stability work) or for relaxation (swimming);
● as additional non-weight bearing (and therefore non-impact) training; for example, if weight loss is a major target or to improve aerobic capacity (always bearing in mind that too much effort may leave you too tired to get full benefit from your main, running based, training sessions);
● to give added variety or when the weather is particularly bad;

● to enhance running performance, and specifically uphill running ability, by cycling.

Cycling

Cycling is well known to have an excellent crossover effect for climbing (running uphill). Many mountain runners include substantial amounts of cycling in their training programme, as both place considerable demands on the quadriceps muscles. The only major downside of cycling is the greater time commitment required to get maximum benefits, unless you are able to do long uphill-only cycling sessions. If using a turbo trainer, running sessions can be replicated on a same time basis with reasonable success.

Some runners also feel that while cycling makes them stronger and better at running uphill, it also makes them slower and tightens the hamstrings (back of the thigh) muscles. These can be alleviated by making sure you keep the pedal revolutions high, include running-based speed sessions and regularly stretch your hamstrings.

Swimming/Pool Work

Swimming has only limited crossover benefits for running, although if swimming hard enough it will improve aerobic fitness. Many runners swim as a method of relaxing on their rest or easy days. More specific running benefits can be obtained from running in the water using a flotation vest. By wearing a flotation device you are able to 'run' in deep water without touching the bottom of the pool, therefore replicating the running action, but with no impact. What scientific studies have been done suggest that if you work hard enough, then deep-water running can certainly maintain, if not improve, running specific fitness.

The easiest way to use deep-water running is to simply replicate the sessions that you would do on land on a time basis in the pool. If therefore you had planned to do efforts of 400m, then run hard in the water for the same amount of time as it would normally take you to do each effort.

Other forms of aerobic exercise can also be used when injured or unable to run to help maintain fitness; in particular cross-country skiing (for real or on a machine) and in the gym the step machine and elliptical trainer.

TERRAIN

Even switching from running on roads to running on grass requires subtle changes in style and running mechanics, as well as altering the work requirements on your stabilizer muscles. It is not uncommon to find two runners of compatible ability when running on one surface (for example, roads) who appear to be of very different standards when running on another terrain (for example, trails). Here the subtle twists, ability to change foot plant and change stride length in mid stride are all essential skills on all but the flattest paths.

Pool Running Tips

- Check with the attendants and other swimmers that it is alright for you to run in the water and which is the best lane (be prepared for people to ask about what you are doing)
- If using a heart rate monitor, expect your heart rate to be approximately 10 per cent lower than on land for any given intensity/session.
- Deep-water running works your upper body harder than running on land due to the water resistance.
- Remember to work on maintaining a correct running action.
- As it is a non-impact exercise, expect to feel tired but not sore after a hard session.

Being good at running on road or track-type surfaces means your body is able to cope with literally thousands of identical foot strikes. The same length, the same landing position, the same conditions under foot, with no obstructions or obstacles to impede your legs or stride pattern, and the resultant identical forces and stresses placed on the body. Part of becoming good at running on the roads is training your body to be able to repeat this movement as efficiently as possible and to do so without injury or breakdown. As a consequence, many top road runners have a near shuffling style.

On off-road surfaces it is different. As well as typically being a softer and therefore more forgiving surface, continual changes in foot-strike and therefore in lower body position are required, as well as a more dynamic running style, being able to bound, hop or jump over rocks at speed. Top fell runners seem to be able to float over knee-deep heather or bracken or run across slippery, uneven, and lose rocks without breaking stride or slowing down. Taking it a step further, orienteering involves running fast through thick undergrowth while using your arms to fight though thick forest, jumping over broken branches and reading a map at the same time.

Running at speed over rougher off-road terrain therefore tends to put greater proprioceptive demands (neural sensations of joint and muscle movement and separation), particularly in the ankle joint and surrounding soft-tissue structures. While using tape to add additional protection and strength to weak or loose ankles is a possibility, much better is to carry out an appropriate strengthening and proprioceptive rehabilitation programme to ensure that such messages are not needed in the first place. However, a few strips of appropriately placed tape can usefully increase feedback from nerve endings in the skin and help improve proprioception.

It is possible to do some related training exercises to enhance your ability to run 'in' terrain, but the best way to improve is to practise 'in' terrain. This includes doing speed-based work. While it is important to do some hard sessions on relatively good surfaces (to improve your basic running speed that you can then take onto terrain), you will also need to do some speed-based sessions on the type of terrain you want to race over. The surface on which you train on will be the surface that you will become good at running on and at the same sort of speeds.

If you cannot get to appropriate terrain to train on, then practising running fast on as rough a ground as possible along with the following will help:

- proprioceptive, mobility and strength exercises for the ankles;
- strength exercises for the quadriceps;
- general full body mobility and small plyometric-type exercises such as hopping, small jumps (including side to side, not just straight line), quick reactive foot movements and so on.

The latter two will help provide the ability to run with a higher knee lift and more bouncy stride when running through heather or bracken, as well as ensure you are able to react to the ever changing underfoot conditions.

HOW HARD?

How hard should you train? How fast should you do your steady runs? What about the speed of your interval sessions or sustained runs? For many runners the best way to discover the answer, to these questions is by feel, trial and error – either theirs alone, or in combination with a coach. Predicted race speed is often used to set the speed of runs or efforts, although this is not easy to do for off-road running given the varying terrain. Advances in modern technology mean that it is now possible to take a more structured and scientific approach to training, in particular by using heart rate information, and to do so without excessive cost. Basic heart rate monitors now cost less than a good pair of training shoes.

This section explains how to find and use your particular heart rate values should you decide to make use of them. If, however, you do not want to go down this route, then do not worry. Heart rate monitors are a fairly new invention and people have been running fast times for much longer than they have been around. If you do decide to incorporate modern technology into your training then:

- Before you buy a heart rate monitor think about and make a list of the things that you want it to do and those you are not interested in. There is no point in paying extra for features that you are never going to use.
- Remember to use your monitor as a tool to help your training, rather than becoming a slave to it. Do not throw 'gut feeling' and intuition out of the window just because you have science. Remember good coaching is an art that uses science, not science alone.
- When thinking in off-road running terms, terrain and topology can have a considerable effect on your heart rate. There will be times when you cannot go any faster, yet your heart rate is below what it 'should' theoretically be for that type of training session, for example on really rough ground or when running downhill. Equally, there will be times when the opposite is true, for example when climbing, either running or walking uphill.

Heart rates (whether resting, maximum, threshold or training zone), like most physiological variables, are very individual things. Everyone is different and this holds true for heart rate. If you decide to use a heart rate monitor it is important to work out your own personal maximum heart rate, as well as your heart rate at LT (the lactate threshold: *see* Chapter 2). Your heart rate at LT will also be very individual and does not occur at the same percentage of maximum for all runners. Therefore even if two runners have the same resting and maximum heart rates, it is still likely that their training heart rates (steady pace, threshold and race pace heart rates) will be different.

Maximum Heart Rate

There are a number of ways of working out your maximum heart rate, of varying accuracy. The best and most accurate way to assess both your maximum heart rate and your different training values is to undergo a physiological test. This will involve running on a treadmill at ever increasing speeds while your heart rate is measured and a series of small blood samples are taken (from which blood lactate values can be obtained). If the speed increases until you are unable to run any further, then not only will the person carrying out the test be able to tell you your threshold pace/heart rate, but also your maximum heart rate. Other heart rate values that might be provided are for easy/recovery running and steady state (that is, long run) pace.

Next in accuracy is the DIY method. Here it is important to remember that any form of maximum stress or exercise test, whether in a laboratory or carried out on your own, is strenuous. If you have any health worries you should consult your doctor first and if you are feeling at all under the weather, have a cold, 'flu or feel excessively tired postpone the session until another day.

DIY testing can be done in a number of ways, as long as you end up with a very high reading/maximum. There are a number of different 'methods' suggested by experts. Following a good warm up, these include:

- 800m test: run 800m hard, jog for 30sec, then go all out for a second 800m. Your maximum heart rate should be reached near the end of the second run.
- Run hard for 4 to 8min with the last 1 to 2min flat out until you can go no further. Going uphill towards the end of the run (but not too steep) often helps to achieve a high heart rate.
- Repeat hills: run hard for about 90sec uphill. Usually four or five efforts flat out up the hill will see you hitting maximum.

Remember all of these methods are strenuous and you must be fully rested both for safety reasons and to get maximum benefit. They are not a form of weekly training; rather, they should be carried out sparingly.

Finally there is the 'rule of thumb' method, which is typically: maximum heart rate = 220 minus your age (although some scientists suggest that 226 minus age is a better estimation for women). It is not uncommon, however, to find individuals with a ten-beat variance (either higher or lower) than that predicted.

It is also important to remember that your maximum heart rate will vary depending upon exercise mode. When swimming it tends to be lower than cycling or running, and runners usually find higher values running than cycling. This is largely explained by differences in the position of the body as well as the amount of muscle mass used. The more upright you are, the smaller the stroke volume and the higher the heart rate needs to be to maintain cardiac output.

Training Heart Rates

Your training heart rate zones are probably more important for training than your maximum heart rate, as they will enable you to not only optimize the training effect of your sessions, but also ensure that the effect you get is the one you want. If you go to a laboratory

Pool Running Tips		
Training type	**Runner 'speak'**	**% of maximum heart rate**
recovery/steady running	easy–steady	60 to 70
aerobic training	steady	70 to 80
LT pace training	hard–sustained	80 to 90
anaerobic efforts	very hard/maximum	>90

for testing these will be determined for you. If not, you can use the accepted 'norms'.

As you get fitter you typically become able to train at a higher percentage of your heart rate before going over the LT. This fact, plus the individuality of heart rates, means that just using the above 'guestimates' may mean that you end up training too hard or too easily, even if you do determine your individual maximum heart rate.

A simpler way of obtaining a fairly accurate heart rate value to equate to your LT pace is to record/note your heart rate during a fairly flat 10km/10 mile race (40 to 80min of hard sustained running). If you pace the race correctly you should find that for the most part your heart rate is fairly steady. This value will also be very close to your LT equivalent.

IF YOU WANT TO KNOW MORE

Hawley, J. and Burke, L. *Peak Performance* (Allen Unwin, 1998)

Norris, C. M., *Back Stability* (Human Kinetics, 2000)

Wilmore, J. and Costill, D. *Physiology of Sport and Exercise* (Human Kinetics, 1999)

For details of physiology laboratories, contact the British Association of Sport and Exercise Sciences (BASES)

Tel: 0113 289 1020.

Website: www.bases.org.uk

CHAPTER FOUR
Supporting Your Training

It is not enough to follow a perfect training routine if your performance is let down by a weakness in another area. This chapter covers three supplementary topics which will be important when training to run off-road: nutrition, overtraining and navigation.

NUTRITION

This section highlights those areas of nutritional (food and fluid) support that are important (and in some cases fairly unique) to some or all of the disciplines that are covered in this book. Chapters 5 to 10 also include information on the nutritional aspects specific to the different disciplines covered in this book. Those seeking a more in-depth look at nutrition for sporting performance are recommended to read Jane Griffin, *Food for Sport: Eat Well, Perform Better* (The Crowood Press, 2001).

Diet and nutritional supplements are often touted as near miracle substances which can enhance a runner's performance. Unfortunately this is not the case and nutritional changes will not make you a better runner – there is no magic food, supplement or drink that will make you run faster. Rather, while 'bad' nutritional habits can adversely affect your performance, optimal or good nutrition will ensure that you are able to maximize your potential.

In the same way that there are no known miracle nutrients or food stuffs that will give you an extra boost, so there are none that, in moderation, will do you harm or are bad for you (allergies and intolerances aside). However, while there may be no foods that are bad for you, there can certainly be bad individual diets.

The start point for optimal nutrition for off-road running is the same as that for endurance performance, namely a varied diet that:

- contains all the essential nutrients in amounts that meet your requirements
- is based on complex carbohydrates (55 to 70 per cent of total energy intake or 8 to 10g per kg body weight), with appropriate amounts of protein (10 to 15 per cent) and fat (30 to 35 per cent);
- includes no more than moderate amounts of alcohol (and not just before or straight after exercise);
- balances energy expenditure with energy intake (if aiming to maintain body weight);
- includes plenty of fruit and vegetables (recommended five servings a day);
- if vegetarian, includes enough good sources of B vitamins and all the essential amino acids;
- is supported by an optimal fluid intake (at least 2 to 3 litres per day, plus whatever is needed to replace fluid lost during exercise);
- does not depend too heavily on 'junk' or non-quality processed foods;
- contains optimal amounts of calcium and iron;
- is ideally based on more frequent smaller meals (three to six), spread throughout the

day, rather than one or two larger ones;
- is based around what works for you and what you like.

Why Good Nutrition?

Good nutrition for any sport, let alone an endurance-based one, is not just about what and how much you eat, but also when you do so. Getting the timing of your food and fluid intake right can have just as great, if not greater, impact on performance than what you eat. In particular, not eating enough either before, during or after exercise can mean that your muscles and/or your brain literally run out of the best form of energy, carbohydrate, and therefore cease to function optimally.

When? What? How Much?

Making sure that you eat at the right time is as important, if not more, than what or how much. Not taking in energy or taking it in at the wrong time can lead to decreases in performance. In particular there are a number of ways that this can occur.

- **Running low on muscle glycogen or 'hitting the wall'.** As you have limited muscle glycogen and blood glucose stores, it is important when exercising for any length of time to keep these topped up as best possible. This means both making sure that your muscle glycogen stores are as full as possible before you start exercising and that you keep your blood glucose levels topped up as possible by taking in solid and/or liquid fuels when exercising.
- **Low blood glucose level or 'bonking'.** It is not just your muscles that need glucose for energy, but your brain as well. While your muscles, if the worse comes to the worse, can slow down and primarily use fat as an energy source, your brain cannot, it needs blood glucose. If your blood glucose level falls, then you are likely to start feeling light-headed and spaced out, as your brain's ability to function optimally is compromised.
- **Sudden surge in insulin.** When food is eaten, it leads indirectly to a rise in the level of insulin in the blood, as part of the food absorption process. This in turn can cause a lowering of the blood sugar level as glucose is absorbed from the blood. Early research suggested that eating food, particular sugary foods, shortly before exercising (30 to 60min beforehand) triggered this action, leading to a decrease in performance due to blunting the rate of fat usage and at times, feelings of light-headedness due to the lower level of blood sugar. More recent research has shown that this is not necessarily the case and that eating during this time period does not cause a fall in performance. However, it is worth remembering that everyone is different and some athletes do have problems if they eat certain foods close to exercising.
- **Not refuelling properly after exercise.** This will mean that you start your next training session or competition with your muscle glycogen stores not fully replenished and therefore with less energy available.

It is important therefore to work out your own personal eating plan, that covers when you should eat, what you should eat and how much. While it is possible to give advice on all these areas, each individual will have their own preference. If you were to look at the food tucked into convenient rucksack pockets at the start of a mountain marathon, or interview a group of cross-country runners about what their favourite pre-race meal is, you would come across a variety of foods and individual preferences, some common to many, some seemingly bizarre, but which work for that person.

Eating Before Exercise

The time interval which you need to leave between eating and taking part in different types of exercise is important. For example it is recommended that you leave between 2 to 4hr between eating and hard exercise or competition. A longer interval would increase the potential of you either feeling hungry during exercise or experiencing lower blood glucose levels. On the other hand, you might find that you can do an easy long run only 20 to 30min after eating a small meal with a low/medium glycemic index (*see* box), such as a bowl of porridge. What you eat will have an effect here, both in terms of glycemic index and type of food. Fats, for example, slow down the absorption process.

Another factor to consider is how much you eat: a large meal will typically take 3 to 4hr to digest, whereas a snack might take only 1hr. Typically the shorter and more intense the race or run, the longer is needed between eating and starting. This is partly because at slower speeds you will be operating at a lower percentage of your maximum and therefore your stomach is able to continue functioning more normally. It is also easier to exercise straight after eating when you are cycling rather than running, because your stomach is not being 'bounced' around so much.

As well as solids, it is worth working out how long before you plan to start exercising you need to stop drinking if you want to avoid having to stop to relieve yourself while training. This is not so much a problem with really long training sessions out in the hills as they are likely to involve a number of stops to re-fuel, change kit or look at the map and so on. Having to stop during a short race or hard speed session is not such a good idea.

As a runner you might therefore find your pre-exercise food routine is something like:

● most races – food 3hr before, fluids up to 1½hr before;

Carbohydrates are divided into two types: complex and simple. Complex carbohydrates are the starchy ones such as bread, pasta, lentils, potatoes, and so on. Simple carbohydrates are found in ordinary or table sugar, fruits, milk and honey. Typically, it was believed that simple carbohydrates were broken down quickly in the body to glucose, and as a result produced a sudden surge in blood glucose levels. Complex ones one on the other hand were believed to take longer and therefore produce a more sustained supply of energy. It is now known that this is not the case, and that the glycemic index (GI) of the food is more important.

The GI is a way of objectively assessing the effect of carbohydrate-based foods on blood glucose levels. A food's GI (on a scale of 0 to 100) is a measure of the rate at which it causes blood glucose to rise. Foods are typically classified as having a low GI (under 55, these cause a slow increase in blood glucose level), a medium GI (55 to 70) or a high GI (over 70, which case a rapid rise in blood glucose). As the table shows there are some apparent 'surprises' compared to the old complex versus simple idea, with a baked potato (complex) having a high GI and chocolate (simple) a low one.

What does this mean for runners? While research in this area is still ongoing, current recommendations concerning foods, their GI value and exercise are:

● before exercise: go for foods with a low GI;
● during exercise: food/drinks with a medium/high GI;
● after exercise: food/drinks with a high GI (the quicker initial rise in blood glucose after eating foods with a high GI enhances muscle glycogen replenishment in the first couple of hours post exercise).

Glycemic Index Values of Different Foods

Type of food	Low GI	Moderate GI	High GI
Drinks glucose	Sugar free drinks	Sports drinks; Fanta™, cola	Lucozade™; drinks
Cereals	All Bran™; muesli; porridge; Fruit & Fibre type	Shreddies™; Sustain; Branbuds	Cornflakes; Cocopops; Rice Krispies; Weetabix; Shredded Wheat
Bread, biscuits and cake	Heavy grain bread such as granary/multi-grain; pitta bread; chapatis; fruit loaf; sponge cake	Fibre-enriched white bread; muesli bars; flapjacks; muffins; digestive biscuits	Brown bread; wholemeal bread; white bread; French sticks; bagels; crumpets; morning coffee biscuits; rice cakes
Potatoes, rice and pasta	Yams; sweet potatoes; basmati rice; noodles; pasta (most types)	New potatoes; boiled potatoes; macaroni	Instant potato; mashed potato; jacket potatoes; chips; brown/white rice
Fruit and vegetables	Apples; dried apricots; banana; cherries; cantaloupe melon; grapefruit; grapes; orange; peach (canned and fresh); pear; plum; apple, orange, grapefruit juice; carrots, peas, sweetcorn	Apricots (canned); pineapple; papaya; squash; sultanas; raisins; pineapple	Parsnips; pumpkins; swede; broad beans; watermelon
Legumes and grains	Baked beans; chick peas; kidney beans; lentils; soya beans; buckwheat; bulgar wheat	Couscous; cornmeal; millet	Tapioca
Snacks	Most chocolate; popcorn; crisps; peanuts	Some chocolate bars such as Mars bars™; taco shells	Jelly babies/beans; corn chips
Sugars	Fructose; lactose	Honey; sucrose	Glucose
Dairy products	Low fat ice cream; milk; yoghurt		Full fat ice cream

Table reproduced by kind permission of Beta Cell Dietitians, Chelsea and Westminster Healthcare NHS Trust.

- hard/steady training – food 2hr before, fluids up to 1½hr before;
- long run or mountain marathon – food 30min before, fluids the same (this will be expanded on in Chapter 10, but given runners will be starting from around 7.30am, being able to eat and set off soon afterwards is important).

> Finally, it is important to note that the GI values for foods are the value for that food on its own. Combining foods will change the GI value of what you eat.

How much and what to eat for your last meal, particularly before a race, is again very individual, both in terms of your last 'main meal', usually the one the night before, and what you eat on actual day before the competition/training session. Typical guidelines include: eating no more than normal (especially the night before); low fat; low fibre/ bulk; high carbohydrate; low GI (pre-exercise); and plenty of fluid.

Perhaps more important are the more practical issues, as well as identifying the food which you feel comfortable training hard or racing on. It is important, both psychologically and physically, that you eat something that you like and makes you feel good, that you know you can digest in the time available (just before a race is not the time to try something for the first time) and is unlikely to cause you stomach problems when exercising. Many runners have either a favourite meal for the night before or a pre-race meal that they like to eat. This might well just be superstition linked to previous good performances, but if it works, stick to it.

Those taking part in longer events (over 90min) might consider trying drinking 500ml or ½ pint of 4 to 6 per cent carbohydrate solution 5 to 10min before the race starts. This will help kick-start the hydrating and refuelling process, but the time pre-exercise is too soon for any insulin surge to occur or for the fluid to pass through to the bladder.

As a runner, breakfast is a very important meal to eat. While some runners are able to run for 60 to 70min straight after getting up and without eating or drinking anything, this is not an ideal situation. While your leg muscles might be fully restocked with glycogen, the supply of energy to the brain might be starting to dip. Your brain never stops working, and while you sleep continues to use around 6g of glucose per hour, all of which must come from the circulating blood glucose. This is turn comes from glycogen in the liver, where some 90 to 70g can be stored. By the end of the night your liver glycogen stores will therefore be lower and so, potentially, will your blood glucose levels. If you do run before breakfast it is very important to make sure that you eat a good carbohydrate-based meal or substantial snack as soon as possible afterwards.

Eating During Exercise

Many runners would not consider eating and perhaps will not even drink during running. For others, both of these will be vital if they are to complete the event, let alone complete it well. For those taking part in events of under 90min there is probably little to be gained from taking in energy (in solid or liquid form), while for under 60min of running taking fluid on board is not usually necessary. These are however general guidelines, which to a degree depend on the conditions, intensity of exercise and individual sweat rates. If, for example, you are doing a hard interval session in the heat, then it is worth having a drink present to use during your recovery periods.

For events over 90min there is likely to be benefit in taking on board energy as well as fluid (they both of course might come from the same source), and the longer the event the more important this becomes. At an extreme, those taking part in continuous multi-day races are likely to need some 6,000 to 10,000kcal per day (as opposed to around 1,700 to 2,200kcal for a sedentary person), most if not all of which needs to be taken in while exercising.

In addition to the specific needs of the different disciplines (covered in the respective chapters), there are some general points to help you work out your 'exercise eating plan' where needed: in other words, on what basis do you do what you do? Training, of course, is a great place to experiment and find out what works and what you can tolerate in terms of eating and drinking. It is also the time to practise what can be described as the fine art of eating and drinking while running hard. Not being able to do so in races, or having to slow down, means lost time.

You should therefore work out:

- how much fluid do you lose and therefore need?
- how much carbohydrate do you need?
- what can you personally handle (volume, type of food, and so on)?
- what are the physiological limitations?

What Should You Be Aiming For?

- Aim for a carbohydrate intake of approximately 60g per hour (or 1g per kg body weight), especially in long (4hr plus) races. This is the maximum that the body can process. Depending on the event this might involve a mixture of solid and liquid sources.
- Begin the refuelling and rehydrating process early: do not wait until the later part of a race or training session to start.
- Fluids should be at a concentration of 4 to 8 per cent carbohydrate (4 to 8g of carbohydrate per 100ml water); above 8 per cent, fluid absorption will be compromised. In hotter conditions go for lower concentrations or increased fluid intake.
- Aim for little and often; ingest small amounts of fluid every 15 to 20min if possible, and fuel at least every hour.

For events where solids will be eaten, what to eat (other than ideally it should be carbohydrate based) is a matter of preference and practicalities. For example:

- Is it practical? For example, bananas are great, but they have a tendency to get squashed quite easily, especially if they are in a tightly packed rucksack or a bumbag which gets fallen on.
- How easy is a particular energy bar to chew while running? Some are best avoided, particularly in colder weather.
- How bulky is it to carry?
- How easy is it to remove from its wrapping while on the move? It is often easier to remove bars from their wrapping and put them in small plastic bags which are kept easily accessible. Always remember to take your rubbish with you and not leave it on the hill.

Typical favourites used by off-road runners include: jelly babies (or similar); energy bars; chocolate bars (Mars, Milky Way and so on); malt loaf; flapjacks; dried fruit; breakfast bars; Nutrigrain-type bars; fig rolls; and energy gels. Remember that energy gels are designed to be taken with fluid, and failure to do so can cause gastrointestinal and other problems.

Eating After Exercise

This is perhaps the easiest section to give advice on, although it is certainly just as important as the other two. Getting your post-exercise refuelling and rehydration right will help ensure that you recover as quickly as possible and are therefore in the best shape for your next training session. Your muscles are most receptive to replenishing their glycogen (carbohydrate) stores in the first couple of hours after exercise, when they are at their emptiest. During this time the rate at which exercised muscle restores its glycogen is at its highest. There is a limit, however, to the amount of carbohydrate that your body can absorb, typically around 1g of carbohydrate per kg body weight. Therefore to optimize the recovery process you should start to eat or drink as soon as possible after you finish exercising. Smart guidelines here are:

- aim for 50g carbohydrate (or 1g per kg body weight) plus moderate protein (which is also thought to be beneficial) in the first 30min;
- after the first 30min, keep up a regular intake over the first couple of hours or until you eat a normal meal;
- eat a normal meal;
- if you find eating straight after running difficult, use energy replacement drinks;
- keep drinking as well as eating: you need to drink 1½ times what you have lost during exercise (*see* below).

Fluid

Food is important, but more so is fluid. Humans can survive for a considerable time without food, but only a few days without fluid. Approximately 50 to 60 per cent of the

What Is 50g Carbohydrate?
banana/jam sandwich: 2 or 3 slices
100g dried fruit
2 medium bananas
8 rice cakes
175g baked potato
3 or 4 tbsp jam or honey
500ml fruit juice
1½ cans soft drink
1½ chocolate bars
1½ sports bars
2 muesli bars
2 scones
1 slice fruit cake
700ml isotonic drink
5 Jaffa cakes
1 bagel and a small glass of orange juice
60g cereal

human body is water (the figure is slightly higher for men as they usually have a greater muscle mass) and a sedentary person needs around 2 to 3 litres of fluid a day. Runners therefore need to drink this, plus 1½ times what they lose during training. And it should not all be fizzy drinks, caffeine and alcohol. Both caffeine and alcohol are diuretics, in other words they stimulate urine output and therefore less of the fluid drunk is actually absorbed into the blood stream. Remember many fizzy drinks also contain caffeine. Habitual caffeine intake such as four to six cups of tea per day does not seem to affect hydration status as long as sufficient appropriate other sources of fluid are drunk as well.

The simple way to make sure that you are hydrated not dehydrated is to check the colour and quantity of your urine. Plenty of it and straw coloured is great, little and dark in colour is not good news. It is possible to get a small 'pee' chart to check, which is available from the address given at the end of this chapter. Thirst, on the other hand, is not a good indicator of hydration status, as you do not tend to feel thirsty until well after you need to drink. The best way therefore to keep hydrated is to drink regularly by sipping through the day rather than just drinking with meals.

Historically many runners never drank in training or racing. Initially, road race regulations did not allow for frequent drink stations (and then they were only allowed in marathons) and even when they did some runners thought it a sign of weakness to drink or else a potential cause of stitch. This also meant that they did not drink in training, in order to help 'train' their body to cope. This, however, is one area where the notion of training something to make it better does not apply. Not drinking in training (and therefore potentially being in a dehydrated state) will not enable you to offset the inherent performance impairment and potential health problems that come with dehydration.

While there are individual differences (men, for example, tend to sweat more that women), it is possible to lose up to 2 litres of sweat per hour in hot conditions when running. To put this into perspective a loss of 2 per cent body weight though sweating (1.5kg (3lb) for a 68kg (150lb) man (one litre = one kg)) can reduce aerobic capacity by up to 20 per cent. Losses of 5 to 6 per cent of body weight (not uncommon in marathon runners) put you at risk of heat-related illness such as heat exhaustion and heat stroke.

Should you therefore drink on all your runs? Probably not, because not only does it take time for what you drink to be absorbed, but on many runs (especially in the cold and shorter runs) you can keep yourself properly hydrated by drinking beforehand and afterwards. Under what conditions you decide you want to drink in training (length of session, weather, ease of drinking and so on) is a personal decision, but the longer the run and the hotter the weather, the more important it will be to drink. In racing it is certainly worth taking advantage of drinks stations in events over 60min in length. However, this is in itself a problem in many off-road events, as most races do not provide such facilities (*see* later).

In terms of what to drink for hydration purposes, water is fine, but some form of sports drink is generally better. If made to the right concentration these will supply energy, and the inclusion of some salt can also help speed up the absorption process. Sports or energy drinks are drinks that contain energy in the form of carbohydrate. They either come ready made (that is, as fluid) or in a powder for you to make up. Ready-made drinks may also contain a number of other substances, for example caffeine, vitamins, minerals, amino acids, herbal extracts and so on, and it is worth checking the label before you buy. Sports drinks can be:

• hypotonic – their concentration is weaker than that of body fluids;
• isotonic – they have the same concentration as body fluids; these provide you with energy while also optimizing fluid replacement;
• hypertonic – they are more concentrated than body fluids; while they can provide you with more energy, the higher concentration means that fluid absorption is not so quick.

Most of the time it is best to go for isotonic drinks. These have a concentration of 4 to 8 per cent carbohydrate and provide a good balance between speed of gastric emptying (getting the fluid from the stomach to the blood stream) and energy provision. Drinks with a greater concentration of carbohydrate might deliver more energy, but at the expense of fast fluid absorption. When deciding what to drink it is therefore important to decide which is the main problem you are likely to face: dehydration or depletion of energy stores.

Many runners prefer to buy energy replacement powder (such as SIS or Maxim) to make into drinks, rather than ready-made drinks. Not only does this allow you to get the exact concentration you prefer, but it is also cheaper. It is also more practical for use during long races, particularly those without outside help, where drinking provision is down to the runner. Here it is standard practice to carry small plastic bags of pre-weighted power (based on the size of your bottle or cup) that can be added to either a water bottle or cup which is filled in streams along the way to give a drink at the right strength.

How much should you drink when running? While it is possible to give some guidelines (the American College of Sports Medicine for example recommend 150 to 300ml every 15min), there are a number of practical and theoretical points that need to be borne in mind:

Making Up Sports Drinks

When making up drinks:

- 1g powder (assuming 95 to 100 per cent carbohydrate) per 100ml of water = 1 per cent solution.
- 10g per 100ml therefore equals a 10 per cent solution.
- To this it is worth adding a pinch of salt, as sodium helps enhance the fluid absorption process.

You do not, however, have to buy special powder to make an energy drink. DIY versions can be made as follows:

- diluted squash: one part squash to four parts water, pinch of salt;
- diluted fruit juice: one part juice to one part water;
- diluted coke: one part coke to one part water (this also gives you caffeine, which some runners find useful, especially in long endurance races where staying awake is an issue);
- 60g of glucose (sugar) to 1 litre of water plus some low calorie squash for flavour, pinch of salt.

- How much do you need? This will vary depending on the temperature, the humidity, plus your own individual sweat rate.
- How much you can absorb? This is theoretically around 800 to 1200ml per hour, but some runners find it very difficult to drink when running and literally have to teach their bodies to be able to cope.
- What is available? A very pertinent point for off-road runners. Trail and mountain races may or may not include drinks stations. If they do, they are unlikely to be found with the same regularity of road races, rather they will be positioned where it is physically possible to put one. Most fell races, and orienteering and mountain marathons do not have drinks stations. This means that where necessary (for example, not in short fell races) other drinking tactics will have to be used. These will be considered in the individual discipline chapters.

Diet for Competition

Many of the key points about eating and drinking before competition have been covered earlier in this chapter. There are, however, a few other things worth remembering, and more importantly, doing.

Fluid and Exercise Summary

- Make sure you are fully hydrated before you start.
- Find out how long before you start exercising you need to stop drinking to ensure that you do not need to stop to urinate while running.
- Think about drinking up to 500ml just before you start running.
- Aim to replace as much as possible of the fluid you lose while running.
- Once you have stopped aim to drink 1½ times the amount of fluid you have lost. You can work this out by weighing yourself – 1kg = 1 litre of fluid.
- Make sure that you are producing plenty of pale-coloured urine, not limited amounts of dark urine.

- The old method of carbohydrate loading involved a long run, followed by three days of low/no carbohydrate, then three days of high carbohydrate. While this is not really necessary, it is important to optimize your muscle glycogen stores for long races. This means little running (or using your leg muscles) and a high carbohydrate diet in the 3 or 4 days before the competition.
- High carbohydrate does not mean high fat or high energy. Unless you are taking part

Drinking during a fell race.

in a 2-day-plus race (such as a mountain marathon) you should not be looking to eat a greater quantity than normal (remember you will be training less), just to include more carbohydrate within your diet.

- If competing in a mountain marathon you might want to think about eating a bit more in the week or so before the race, as you will probably be operating on an energy deficit during the race itself.
- The week before a race is not the time to experiment. Make sure you are happy with both the timing and content of your meals over the last couple of days. For example, suddenly switching from eating your main meal on the day before a race from the evening to lunchtime is not too clever. While it may give your body more time to absorb the food, it also is quite likely to play havoc with your digestive system (which may already be a bit nervous), ending in diarrhoea or constipation and subsequent problems during the race.
- If travelling to a race, take any favourite or lucky foods with you as you may not be able to find them when you arrive. If the race is abroad, make sure that you check you are allowed to take the food into the country you are visiting.
- Take a post-race snack and drink with you. Food options following off-road events can vary from excellent to non-existent.

OVERTRAINING OR UNDER-RECOVERY?

What is running to you? A way of relaxing? Something that gets put before all else? A major part of your life? A social occasion that allows you to relax and have a good time? A chore that you include in your routine in order to keep fit? Running can be all of these and more. For a few atheletes it is their profession, the way in which that they pay the mortgage. For most (certainly in terms of off-road running), it is just a hobby. Hobbies

can, however, be to all extents a profession (albeit an unpaid one) or can become an obsession.

And here lies the danger: on the one hand, to improve you have to train hard, but train too hard and the consequences can be worse than not training hard enough. Getting the balance right is vital if you want to maximize your performance: fail either way and you will not get the best out of yourself. Many top runners liken this to trying to balance on a thin red line: too little training and you do not improve; too much (or not enough recovery, a subtle but significant difference) and you fall off the other side of the line. When this happens, the decline in both performance and health can be catastrophic, with a slight increase too far leading to a much larger fall off in performance. To recover, you will have to ease right off and normally go further back before you can start the recovery build-up again. And it is not just training that needs to be taken into account, but all forms of stress – physical, social, family, work, relationships, travel and so on.

Stress and the Zulus

While it may be that for you running is not about training as hard as possible without going over the top, it is still important to remember that your body does not compartmentalize stress – stress is stress, whatever the source. It is therefore very important that you are able to balance the forms of stress that affect you. For example, if you have to work particularly long hours one week on a stressful project think about easing back on your training so that it becomes a relaxant rather than a stressor. Training therefore becomes easy 'run as you feel' running rather than trying to stick to a rigid schedule with hard interval sessions (another stressor) at the end of a 12-hour day.

While it might be theoretically possible to fit both work and hard training in to your life,

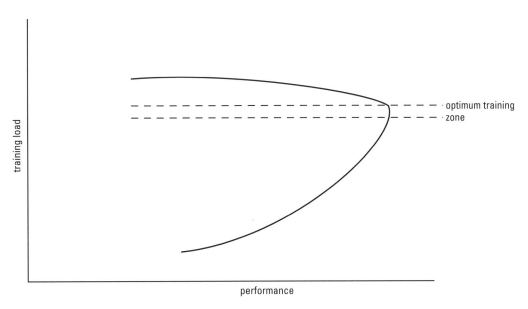

Training load versus effect on performance.

what is in danger of being lost is good quality recovery and relaxation time. It is actually not that difficult to work 50 to 60 hours per week and run 100 miles per week. However, for most people the likely consequence of trying to do both is at best feeling very tired, run down and susceptible to colds and other infections and, at worse, leading to more serious under-recovery problems.

Runners and other athletes often wonder why they do not perform as well and feel tired after travelling, especially flying, even if it does not involve crossing over time zones. Travelling, while possibly not a great physical stress, is a stress none the less and one that your body needs to be allowed to recover from. This will not happen unless you make allowances in your training by adding some additional recovery time or easy training sessions.

Another way of thinking about your body and stress is the Zulu principle, first developed by Professor David Collins. This is based on the film of the same name ('Zulu'), in which a fort is surrounded by Zulus, all intent on overrunning the fort and killing the defenders. Now think of yourself as the fort and all the stresses in your life as the Zulus: you can cope as long as there are not too many Zulus (stressors). In this case your defenders, such as the immune system, psychological coping skills and so on, are able to repel the invaders. This represents, hopefully, the status quo of normal life.

What happens when the Zulus (stressors) increase? As long as they behave correctly and only attack one point of the fort, things are usually manageable. When this happens, the defenders are able to use all their resources to concentrate their efforts at the point where the Zulus are attacking and keep them at bay. This obviously means that the fort's defences are weakened elsewhere, as there are only a limited number of defenders. This is not a problem, until the Zulus realize and decide to attack in force from all directions. The result? The fort's defences cannot cope and the fort is overrun.

So what does this mean in practice and, more importantly, how can we prevent the

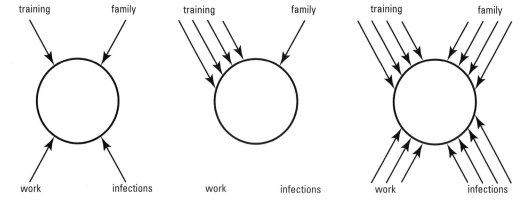

Stress attackers on the system/fort.

Zulus from winning? There are three possibilities here. First, limit the overall number of stressors: a good example of this might be the full-time runner who removed the work stressor by resigning from work. Secondly, learn to recognize when stresses are high in one area and therefore decrease other pressures. Think back to our previous example of having to cope with extra work pressures and still trying to train hard – this would mean that the pressures are high from a couple of areas. Decreasing the training stressors can help ensure that the fort's defences are able to cope and not be defeated. Finally, you can recruit more defenders by being pro-active in terms of your nutrition, sleep and other areas such as applied psychology techniques, or for regular blood testing and so on.

The alternative is that too much stress is put on the body, leading to some form of eventual breakdown (feeling overtired, suffering from colds, influenza, cold sores, or being run down), and fall off in performance (in both work and running). The message from this is simple: be aware of what pressures you are under. Or, put another way, keep an eye on your personal Zulus!

It is also important to recognize that how much stress (or Zulus) we can cope with and how we react to different forms of stress are very individual. Just because your training

partner can cope with something does not mean that you will be able to. Nor does admitting that you cannot cope with training hard and only getting 6 hours sleep a night mean that you are 'weak' or not as 'hard', just different in how your body reacts (and more sensible).

Unexplained Underperformance Syndrome

What, however, happens should you unfortunately fail to keep the Zulus out, particularly the training ones? Getting the correct balance to your training is not easy. Hard training is needed to improve, but too much and underperformance, not improvement, can occur. It is estimated that unexplained underperformance affects some 10 to 20 per cent of elite endurance athletes.

The unexplained underperformance syndrome (or UPS for short) is a fairly new term created to explain symptoms that have previously been described as, amongst others, going over the top, burn out, staleness, overtraining syndrome, and chronic fatigue. UPS better reflects what scientists feel is more likely to be the problem; one of under recovery from training rather than too much training. In other words, these types of problems are more likely to be brought about by insufficient rest and recovery, rather than too much hard training. This is why it is important to ensure that within your training programme you include both hard sessions and easy rest/recovery ones. Try thinking of a rest day as a recovery training session. Monotonous (same intensity), heavy, training programmes on the other hand are more likely to lead to UPS-type problems.

UPS has been defined as 'a persistent unexplained performance deficit (recognized and agreed by coach and performer) despite two weeks rest'. As well as underperformance there are a number of symptoms associated with UPS, some or all of which might be present.

While there are some procedures that runners can use to try to monitor their training state to prevent UPS occurring, as of yet there is no single infallible measure. Possible indicators are:

- blood measures (which require medical assistance);
- morning heart rate: this tends to rise by up to 10 beats per minute when you are over tired and not fully recovered from previous training, and it can therefore be a useful sign that your body needs a bit more recovery;

- mood state profiling: the onset of UPS tends to be accompanied by feelings of depression, feeling down and not so keen to train.

Some runners now use their training diary to record and monitor not only the training they do, but also things like training quality, how they felt, mood, hours slept, weight, heart rate and so on, in order to try and catch any potential onset of UPS at an early stage.

If you are unfortunate enough to suffer from UPS (and it can affect anyone, not just the elite), then there is really only one known cure: rest or at least recovery. First, however, it is important to check with your GP to ensure that nothing more serious or explainable is wrong. A period of very light exercise (starting at 5 to 10min per day and building up slowly, heart rate no more than 140bpm and preferably using cross training (in other words, if you are a runner, not running)) for 6 to 12 weeks is usually enough to kick-start the recovery process.

Once this point is reached, it is important to remember all is not yet back to normal, and to continue to build up slowly, carefully monitoring your body and making sure that it gets enough rest. The alternative may be to fall into a vicious cycle of partial recovery.

Symptoms Associated With UPS

The following symptoms have been associated with UPS:

- fatigue and unexpected sense of effort during training;
- history of heavy training and racing;
- frequent minor infections;
- heavy, stiff and sore muscles, loss of energy;
- mood disturbance;
- change in expected sleep quality;
- loss of appetite;
- loss of libido;
- loss of competitive drive.

NAVIGATION

You will have to come to grips with navigation if you are going to do any more than the most urban off-road running. Runners who just want to add off-road running to their repertoire to get the benefits in training will probably be able to get away with just knowing how to use a map. If you are thinking about taking part in fell running, mountain marathons, orienteering or just running in the hills then compass work becomes important. This section looks at the basics you will need, but for further training exercises *see* Chapter 9.

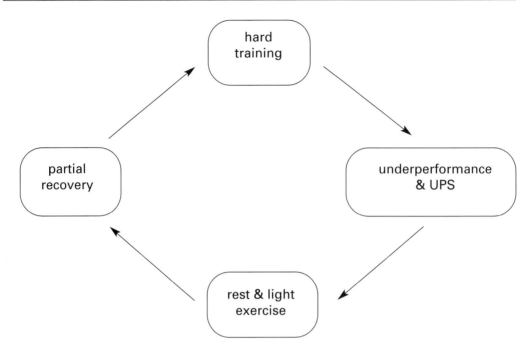

The cycle of partial recovery.

The Map

Understanding the Map

In Britain we are spoilt with the quality and range of maps available, something that becomes apparent when travelling abroad. Most runners will be familiar with the pink 1:50,000 (2cm = 1km) Landranger series of maps produced by Ordnance Survey (OS), which cover the whole country. OS also produce 1:25,000 maps (4cm = 1km); yellow Outdoor Leisure double-sided maps cover areas of outstanding natural beauty, while orange Explorer ones will soon cover the rest of the country (the content of these two in terms of symbols is the same). Scale apart, switching between the different OS maps is not difficult as most of the symbols and colourings used, as well as the contour lines, are the same. Contour lines are used to show the height above sea level, and on OS maps they are every 10m.

Harvey's maps, which are designed for recreational use, mainly covering popular walking areas and long distance trails, are another choice. Harvey's Walkers' maps are 1:40,000 scale (2.5cm = 1km), with contours every 15m. They also produce a Superwalker series on a scale of 1:25,000. At first glance a Harvey's map can look quite intimidating to those used to OS maps, both from the actual 'look' of the map, as well as the different symbols and colour shades used. However, many runners prefer them, not least because the scale is compatible to that required for mountain marathons, as well as the level of detail shown. When using a particular type of map for the first time, or when re-equating yourself with one, it is worth spending some time checking the map legend which explains the various symbols, paths and roads and ground coverings, as well as the scale.

To use a map successfully it is important to be able to interpret it: do you know what all the symbols and coloured lines mean? It is not unknown for runners to set off trying to follow a parish boundary line expecting it to be a footpath. You will also need to be able to work out where you are on the map and to follow your progress as you move. Here it is not just the features which are important, but also having an understanding of the scale of the map and the use of contours and what this means 'on the ground'.

Grid lines appear on all British maps, with one set running directly north–south and the other west–east. The lines are set by the British National Grid and are spaced 1km apart (and are therefore helpful for estimating distances). As each line has a two figure number (given on the side of the map, as well as sometimes on the grid lines as well), it is possible to give a fairly accurate six figure reference for a particular feature. Any feature will always have the same grid reference whether on a Harvey's, OS or other map. Grid references (which are used to give the position of checkpoints in fell, orienteering and mountain marathon events) are always read east/west then north/south or, put in another way, along then up.

Contours show the height of the land

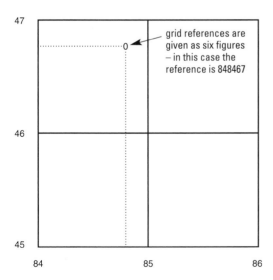

Plotting a grid reference on a map.

above sea level, with all the points on a contour line being at the same height. For experienced map readers a quick glance at the contour lines, how close together they are and their patterns, can provide an extremely accurate virtual 3D picture of the actual terrain, giving a picture of how steep it is, how high and its shape. Those new to map use may find it difficult enough to tell the difference between going uphill and down. Taking longer with the map will clarify this. Maps have index contours, which are thicker and give the actual height on them (on OS maps these are every 50m and on Harvey's every 75m). Remember, rivers and lakes will tend to be found in dips, and cairns and summits on the tops of features.

Using the Map

Having a good grasp of the basic concepts discussed above will help tremendously in making sure you maintain contact with your position on the map and therefore do not get lost. When setting out, you should fold the map in such a way that you can see where you are, and preferably at least some of your planned route. This might sound obvious, but many runners just put the unopened map in their bumbag. The map should then be set with the ground. To do this, stand facing the direction in which you plan to run and orientate the map so that it is facing the same way and the features on the map match those on the ground. Looking at the map should now make sense when compared to what can be seen in the direction where you plan to go.

When heading off on a training run, especially if slightly familiar with the area, many runners then put their map in their bumbag, stopping when needed to check where they are and which route to take. In orienteering and mountain marathons as well as some fell races, keeping in contact with the map at all times is essential. The best way to do this is to hold the map all the time, 'thumbing' it. This means keeping your thumb next to your posi-

Setting the map with the ground and thumbing it. Figure adapted with kind permission from M. Bagness, Mountain Navigation for Runners *(Misty Fell Books, 1993).*

tion on the map, maintaining map contact at all times. Even if you have to stop to double-check, you will not waste time searching the map to find where you are on it.

If using a map to plan training routes, make sure that you are familiar with the symbols used to represent a path, bridle way, right of way and so on, compared to a fence, railway line or boundary. The OS and Harvey's maps use different colours for these. It is important that you know which is which and stick to where you are allowed. Not only for safety reasons (boundary lines can go over inaccessible cliffs) but also to prevent trespassing. The later is especially true if cross training on a mountain bike.

Even experienced map readers still make mistakes when out in the field, especially under race pressure. As with any skill, practice, including 'armchair' map reading, will help.

The Compass

In 'easier' terrain, good weather and when on well-defined paths, a map may be all that is needed. There are other times when having and using a compass will be essential. Even on well-trodden paths in the Lake District, once the mist is down it is easy to become disorientated or lose the path. You only need to go slightly off course to either lose time (if racing) or, more seriously, end up in some kind of trouble.

The good thing about compasses is that, all things considered, they do not lie. Therefore if you think south is one way and the compass points another, trust the compass. The only times when this might not be the case will be if the compass is damaged or the magnetic needle affected. The latter can occur in some parts of Scotland.

A compass works on magnetic bearing: the red part of the arrow always points north. Just knowing this can sometimes be enough to help with navigation: you can work out where north is, and therefore re-orientate yourself accordingly.

Setting the Compass

Setting the compass with the map is a step on from setting the map with the ground. If you know where you are on the map, this will help make sure that you go in the right direction. The compass is placed on the map (usually holding both in the same hand) with the base plate parallel to the direction you want to go in. Think about drawing an imaginary line between where you are and the feature you want to get to. The map and compass are then rotated together until the compass needle (the red end) is aligned with the north–south grid lines on the map pointing north. The direction of travel arrow on the compass baseplate is now pointing in the direction in which you need to go. Orienteers, especially if using a thumb compass, will tend to run with the map and compass set the whole time.

Taking and Using a Bearing

When first tried, taking a bearing can seem a little daunting and confusing, especially in the mist, on a hill and when the direction you

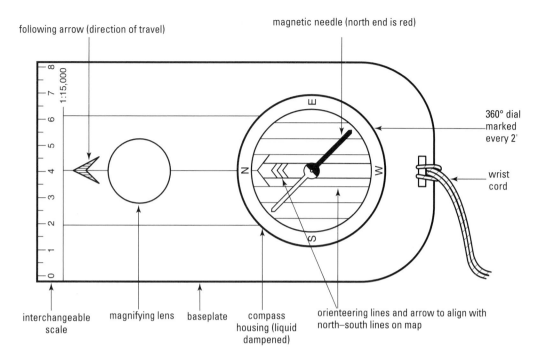

following arrow (direction of travel)

magnetic needle (north end is red)

360° dial marked every 2'

wrist cord

interchangeable scale

magnifying lens

baseplate

compass housing (liquid dampened)

orienteering lines and arrow to align with north–south lines on map

Line drawing of a base plate compass.

arrive at 'seems wrong'. With a little practice, however, the technique should soon become ingrained and invaluable. What does taking a bearing mean? And, more importantly, what does it allow you to do? If you know where you are on the map and where you want to get to, taking a bearing is a more accurate way of finding the direction you want to go using the map and compass. Taking a bearing is based on measuring the angle between north (0°) and your line of travel. The most common way of doing this is known as the four-stage method, which is shown pictorially.

Usually a bearing is taken because you cannot see the feature you are heading for or because the mist is down. Once it is taken you have two options. You can run 'on the needle', in other words, run holding the compass in the flat of your palm following the direction of travel. However, even with a modern quick setting compass this is not easy, partly because the needle moves around, and also because you will have to try to look in two places at once (or fall over). Much better is to use visible objects along the way. Once you have the bearing, hold the compass level and steady, giving enough time to let the needle settle. Pick out an object some distance away on the line of travel (such as a large boulder or tree), ensuring that you will be able to see it the whole time as you run to it. Run to the feature, then repeat the process, at the same time making sure that you can follow your progress on the map.

Other Useful Techniques

If you can read a map and use a compass you are probably covered for most eventualities. There are a few other general skills that can come in useful, especially if you need to locate checkpoints in a race.

Pacing, or knowing how many steps (single or double) you take to cover a certain

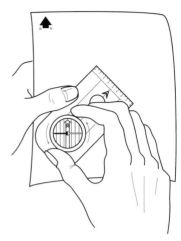

1. Place the compass on the map with the edge of the base plate alongside the line you wish to follow.

2. Rotate the housing until the housing arrow is aligned with the north lines on the map.

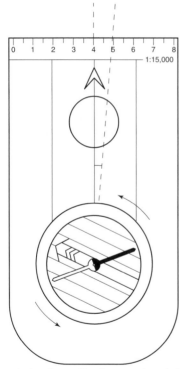

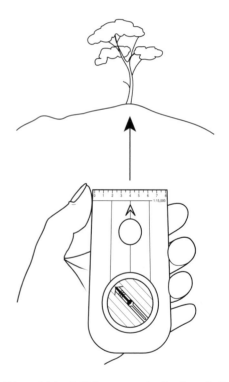

3. Rotate the housing to allow for magnetic variation (i.e. between magnetic north and true north). This varies with time and place: the relevant data will be found in the map legend.

4. Take a sighting: hold the compass level and steady. Turn the whole compass and yourself until the needle is aligned with the housing arrow. The compass is pointing in your direction of travel.

The four-stage method for taking a bearing. Figure reproduced with kind permission from M. Bagness, Mountain Navigation for Runners *(Misty Fell Books, 1993).*

distance (say 100m) is useful, particularly if the conditions and terrain are such that it is difficult to finely align your position from map to terrain, for example, if you know there is an indistinct path off a summit about 100m away. Pace counting means that you know when you are 100m from the summit and can then look much more carefully for the path. Orienteers often have a number of different pace scales, covering fast running, running in terrain or really thick forest.

Another skill useful for distance estimation and working out how far you have run is to know approximately how long you normally take to cover 1km in rough terrain. And in addition, how much time you should add to this for every 10m climbed.

If running between two points with either a hill or a valley in between, is it better to go up and down or round? The straight line up and down route will be shorter, but will it be quicker? Here, **route choice** becomes important. If you are interested in doing well in events requiring navigational skills, then it is not just enough to know where you are, you also need to be able to choose the best route. As well as the difference between the extra distance going round and the extra height climbed (a rough rule of thumb is 50m climbed equates to 500m on the flat), there are a number of other things to take into account (and not simply which way the other runners are going).

Again, the best way to improve your route choice is to practise, both on the hills and at home by studying maps and working out which way you would go and why.

If you are trying to find a small feature or checkpoint that is not obvious (such as a stream junction or re-entrant rather than a small hill summit), and which may be some distance away, then using what are known as **handrails** and an **attack point** are worthwhile.

When running from one control or place to another, handrails are distinct features on the way that you can use to check your exact position with the map. These are particularly useful when the two places are quite far apart. Use of key handrails can also reduce the amount of time you spend stopping to look at the map. For example if you know you have to cross a track, then you can confidently run on a bearing until you hit it before re-engaging with the map.

An attack point is an obvious, easy to find feature or point near to the control you are trying to find. When you reach that point you know exactly where you are, and in what direction the control is.

Everyone gets lost on the hills at some point, usually when the mist comes down. This is when being able to **relocate** and work out where you are comes in handy. The first thing to do is set the map and compass (and yourself), with each other, and ideally the ground as well so that they are correctly orientated. This way the map matches the ground and you are facing what should be your direction of travel. Now try to match

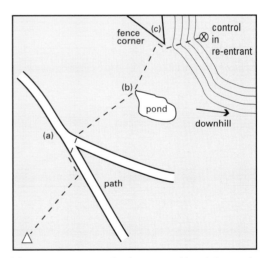

(a): Hand rail – take bearing from start to hit path; from path junction take bearing to pond

(b): Hand rail – pond corner, take bearing from end to left side of fence (to make sure you do not overshoot)

(c): Attack point – fence corner, fine bearing and pacing downhill to control

Handrails and attack points.

How to Decide Which Route to Take

- What is the estimated extra distance versus climb?
- Are there any paths that you can run on?
- Is there a good final attack point?
- What is the terrain underfoot like?
- Does the terrain suit your style of running?
- What about the weather? (Is it best to avoid exposed ridges?)
- Are there good handrails on the way?
- How are you feeling?
- Would one route give you time to recover, look at the map and plot the rest of the course?

features on the ground (ones you can see), with those on the map. If this is possible you can then either run to the feature, in which case you are no longer lost, or take what is called a **back bearing** to help find your exact position. If there are two or more identifiable features, then taking two or three back bearings should provide a series of lines which intersect where you are on the map.

If you cannot clearly identify a feature on the ground, think about when you last knew exactly where you were. It may be that you have to retrace your steps, carefully on a bearing, until you are again 'not lost'. Alternatively you can try to work out where you are on the map by tracking the direction of travel from your last known point (assuming you were on an accurate bearing) and estimating how far you have run since you were there. Once you have a rough idea where you are on the map, you can either use the back-bearing method to try and pin-point your position, or select a very definite feature on the map (such as a fence, hill or road) and follow a compass bearing towards it.

Finally, when running with a compass it is worth attaching it to your wrist with a cord. The last thing you want to do is drop it down a gully when suddenly having to use both hands for balance!

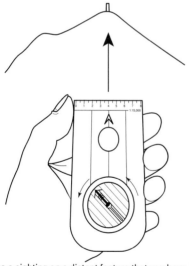

Take a sighting on a distant feature that you have identified on the map. Turn the housing until the housing arrow is aligned with the north needle. Rotate the housing to allow for magnetic variation (data for which will be on your map's legend)

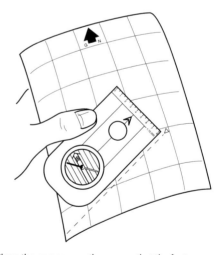

Place the compass on the map so that the feature you sighted on is on the edge of the base plate. Turn the compass so that the housing arrow is aligned with the north lines on the map. Your position will be somewhere on a line along the side of the base plate, passing through the feature you sighted on.

Taking a back-bearing. Figure reproduced with kind permission from M. Bagness, Mountain Navigation for Runners *(Misty Fell Books, 1993).*

With time and practice it is likely that you will work out which technique (map/ground features, compass, distance estimation) you tend to use most and is your preferred method of navigation. Remember, however, there will be some occasions when the methods you are perhaps not so strong on will be needed. As with physical training, you should make a point to work on your weaknesses.

IF YOU WANT TO KNOW MORE

Griffin, J. *Food for Sport: Eat Well, Perform Better* (The Crowood Press, 2001). Much of the factual information contained in this chapter has been taken from this title.

Credit-card sized 'Pee' charts are available from Dietitians in Sport and Exercise Nutrition, PO Box 22360, London, W13 9FL.

FHS *Preventing Underperformance* (Coachwise Ltd, July 2000). The section on overtraining or underperformance is based on an article by Richard Budgett, which first appeared in issue 8, July 2000.

Bagness, M. *Mountain Navigation for Runners* (Misty Fell Books, 1993).

The Fell Runners Association run weekend navigation courses twice a year (*see* Chapter 7 for contact details).

CHAPTER FIVE
Trail Running

WHAT IS TRAIL RUNNING?

Broadly speaking, trail running is running on surfaces other than tarmac roads. Depending on availability this can include grass, canal paths, sand, wooded paths, open moorland tracks, dirt roads and woodchip trails.

During the late 1990s, trail running was the biggest growth area of the sport as previous road runners discovered the added benefits of running on what for most is typical 'off-road' terrain. To say trail running is a new discovery is, however, wrong. For years, many experienced distance runners have used the softer, more forgiving, off-road surfaces to train on, even if their racing priorities were on the roads and track.

Of all the forms of off-road running, trail running is probably the most common worldwide and runners travelling abroad can find delightful trails to run on – around Finnish lakes, up Alpine mountain trails, in the Australian outback and the North American Rockies. As long as you remember to take appropriate safety precautions, running on

---

Safety Precautions When Running Abroad

- Is it safe to run, considering risks from both humans and animals (such as snakes)? Are you likely to upset local traditions or cultures?
- Do you need a map? Take a map case or plastic bag, as this will save your map from being ruined by rain or sweat.
- If a map is necessary, make sure that you have the basic skills to be able to use it.
- Do you need a compass? Again, make sure you know at least how to find north and south, and that your compass is the right one for the country you are visiting. Note that British compasses will work in Europe and North America, but not Australia.
- If you are running alone, it is good practice to tell someone where you are going and what time you expect to be back.
- If running in isolated places take a whistle, as this is invaluable if you are injured and need to call for help.
- Check that you are allowed to run where you

plan to go. In some old Eastern European countries the authorities can be suspicious about individuals carrying maps and cameras, especially if running near military-type buildings or land.
- If you are likely to be running in isolated or exposed areas think about taking some lightweight windproofs with you in a bumbag. While you may be warm enough when running, if you have an accident and either have to walk or call for help you will chill off quickly.
- Consider taking some coins for use in a phone box in emergencies or carrying a mobile phone. If you are carrying a phone, put it in a plastic bag to avoid sweat and, of course, check that it will operate in the area in which you are running.
- Depending on the length of your planned run and the local environmental conditions, do you need to take any fluid or food with you?

---

trails is a great way to see more of the countries you visit, usually in less polluted air and on terrain that is kinder to your body.

While trail running can take place worldwide, it does not mean that all trails are equally well defined and of similar terrain under foot. Even in Great Britain, a designated footpath shown on an Ordnance Survey map can mean very different things when you try to run over it 'on the ground'. It is usually not until you get there that you find out whether it is a decent trail to run on, a seemingly imaginary line to follow across a corn field, or a loose, rocky path. This is something that is exacerbated abroad, especially in countries where the maps are not of the same standard as the Ordnance Survey or Harvey's. So, be prepared the first time you venture onto a particular trail: it might turn out to be great for fast running, but on the other hand it might be such that you are reduced to a walk, jog or scramble.

Whatever type of trail or any other off-road running appeals to you, remember the importance of not only leaving the countryside as you found it (assuming that you found it in a good state), but also respecting those who own or use the land. It is worth reminding readers of the Country Code and the importance of sticking to it while out running.

The Country Code

Fasten all gates.
Keep to public paths across farmland.
Guard against fire risks.
Use gates and stiles to cross fences, hedges and walls.
Leave livestock, crops and machinery alone.
Take your litter home.
Help keep water clean.
Protect wildlife, plants and trees.
Take special care on country roads.
Make no unnecessary noise.

To which can be added: if running with a dog (or other animal) always make sure that it is kept under control and does not pose a threat to livestock, wildlife, walkers or other runners.

COMPETITIONS

Just like trail running, trail races cover a wide range of experiences. At one end are good flat surfaces where running speeds will be similar to those on the roads; at the other some trail races would qualify as C standard fell races. Some trail races are as well organized as any road races, others are much more informal and laid-back affairs. Distances also vary, from very short to very long or ultra endurance events. Races are also frequently over odd or rough distances rather than the exact 10km or 10 miles more typically found on the road. The Trail Running Association, which oversees the sport in Britain, initially only catered for ultra distance events, but now covers all distances. Races are normally held on footpaths, bridlepaths and towpaths (that is, public rights of way).

Like many forms of off-road running, trail running tends to be less pressurized and lower key than road racing. There is a national trail running championships, with races over distances of 9 miles, 'marathon' and 44 miles. It is probably fair to say, however, that these do not have the same status as major events in the other disciplines. The downside of this less formal approach are the shorter and less valuable prize lists and fewer finishing momentos, the upside is that they are frequently more friendly and cheaper.

As well as 'formal' trail races, many other organizations such as the Long Distance Walkers Association are happy for runners to take part in their events. These do not normally have prizes or even results. They will however have a set route (not always marked), often with refreshments on the way and a great atmosphere.

Running along the canal, Burnley Urban 10km race.

For those looking further afield there are numerous long-distance trail/mountain type races in Europe and North America, particularly over either 50 or 100 miles, for example the Western States 100 miles and the Vermont trail. This area is also covered in Chapter 8.

Trail races are typically held over marked courses and therefore do not require route choice, navigational skills or pre-race reconnaissance. This would still be useful even for marked courses as it not only enables you to find out what the terrain is like underfoot, but also where any stiles, narrow bits or sharp turns (and therefore potential bottlenecks) will be found, as well as where the steep up and down hills occur.

The fact that the course is marked does not mean that it is not possible to go wrong. The very nature of trail races means that they tend to take place in surroundings that are not always easy to mark or marshal, with plenty of twists and turns from one path to another, and previously set out signs may go 'astray'. It is always worth having a good look at the course map beforehand (if available) especially when running a particular race for the first time. Once the race is underway, remember to keep a sharp eye out for the next bit of tape tied to a branch, rather than just relying on following the runner in front.

The rough and varied nature of trail races means that it is more difficult to estimate how long a particular race will take based on distance alone. It is therefore helpful to find out what the winning times for men and women have been in previous years, as well as the slowest times. This will give you a better estimation as to how long you are likely to take. Do not expect to find accurate mile or kilometre markers along the route: more often than not there will not be any, or if they have been given they will be attached to the nearest convenient tree or post. Likewise, drinks stations may or may not be present. If they are present, they are more likely to be based at a place which is easy and convenient to get supplies to, rather than at a predetermined distance into the race. When registering at the race it is always worth checking details of any drinks stations with the race organizer. If you are in any doubt about the amount of fluid which will be available on the course, you should consider carrying your own drink with you.

Given the possibility of very different types of terrain underfoot, which will also be affected by the weather, it is always worth taking both road racing type trainers as well as more-studded trail or fell running shoes to races. A quick look at the start and finish of the course, plus a word with the organizer or other runners will help you decide which type is best suited to that course on that day. It is not unusual to find a trail race one year is run over a wet muddy course best suited to studs, but the next year has a bone dry and hard packed surface ideal for racing flats. Using flats on a muddy wet course or studs on a bone-dry hard course will not only potentially be disadvantageous in terms of performance but may increase the risk of injury.

KIT AND EQUIPMENT

Trail running does not require any additional kit or equipment – your usual off-road running kit should be sufficient. However, there are a few items to consider.

Socks

If you are running on anything other than very good trails in dry weather you are likely to end up with wet or muddy socks and the potential for cold and wet feet. A number of manufacturers now sell dark coloured socks that do not show the mud stains. *See also* Chapter 7.

Bumbag

If you are likely to be running in isolated or exposed areas it is often worth carrying a set of lightweight windproofs or an additional top and hat in a bumbag in case of emergencies. The bumbag also means that if you take a map, you do not have to carry it in your hand the whole time.

Shoes

It might come as a surprise that although runners have been enjoying the benefits of off-road running for years, it is only fairly recently that there have been specialist trail or off-road running trainers. Now any self-respecting running or fitness company produces a number of trainers designed specifically for the off-road running market. Are they needed? A lot of the time, the honest answer has to be 'no'. Especially in dry conditions, most trail surfaces are suitable for road shoes which have a slight studded or waffle-type sole. These also have the advantage that you can mix surfaces without worry, which is useful considering that it is probably quite rare to run totally on trails in any one run. If ordinary running shoes are fine for some trail running, what are the advantages or disadvantages of specialist trail shoes?

- **Grip.** The major plus for trail running shoes is extra grip, as a result of a more deeply lugged or studded sole. While this might not seem so important if you run on flat canal bank type surfaces, over wet fields in winter it will make a considerable difference. Good grip on muddy terrain does not, however, equal good traction on wet, flat surfaces; here the type of rubber used plus smaller amount of actual contact between the shoe and ground (via the studs) can mean a very slippery ride on smooth, wet, pavements.

- **Outer.** Most trail shoes have a tough upper, often with a 'stone protector' over the toes. While these do give the shoes more protection against rocks and thick scrub, think carefully how important this is to you compared to the resultant additional weight and loss of flexibility. A number of trail shoes are now made of Gore-Tex or other water-resistant fabrics, again making the shoe heavier and also warmer.
- **Cushioning.** Trail shoes typically have less cushioning than road ones. While many are designed for training on a mixture of surfaces, others are best suited to totally off-road running.

When thinking about what shoes to wear for trail running, two other points are worth considering, particularly if you plan to run on rougher trails.

- **The width of the shoe.** If your feet are able to move around from side to side in the shoe, something which is likely to happen on rough terrain, the potential for blisters on the sides of your feet is increased. A reasonably tight fitting shoe is therefore usually better.
- **The height of the heel.** Some running shoes have a low heel height, meaning that your foot is closer to the ground. Others have a higher, often flared, heel. While in principle, this might seem preferable, in practice on rough uneven ground there is a greater likelihood that the shoe will be unstable, with increased potential for twisted ankles.

TRAINING

Training for trail running does not really differ from that for road running. There are no specific types of training sessions over and above those you would normally do based on the distance of the event(s) you are training for. What is more important is to try and do at least some of your training on surfaces similar to those that you will be racing over.

NUTRITION

As with training, trail running does not really require any specific nutritional changes or additions over and above good endurance-orientated nutrition. Compared to races on the road you may have to consider hydration while running more carefully. In training, if you do not go past suitable places to take fluid on board, this might mean running with fluid. As well as the more common handheld bottles, a number of companies now make waist belts designed to carry water bottles whilst running, and for really long runs you might consider using a camel back water carrier.

In races where drinks stations are likely to be sited based on ease of access, not best timing for runners, it is important to make sure that you take full advantage of what is available. Some long distance trail races may also have food available. Depending on the length of the race and the rules, outside assistance in the form of fluid provided by helpers may be allowed. This can vary from a friend or relative giving you a drinks bottle at a particular spot on the course, to ultra events where runners have mobile back-up teams. In long races like the Birmingham to London Grand Union Canal race or the South Downs Way, most runners will have some form of personal back-up team. They will aim to meet the runners at set points along the route to provide food, fluid, kit changes and much needed encouragement.

Runner Biography: Mark Croasdale

Mark winning the Lancashire Cross Country Championships 2001.

Despite all he has achieved, Mark Croasdale is perhaps best known for something he nearly did. In 2000, he took on a horse and over 20 miles lost out by only 80sec. The Man verus Horse race in Wales has long offered a prize of over £20,000 to the first runner to beat the horses and win the race outright. Mark has won the race five times, coming closest to the horse in 2000. When he has not won the race as an individual, he has done so as part of the 'Croasdales Crusaders' four-man relay

Runner Biography: Mark Croasdale *continued*

team (six times), including beating the horse.

As a young lad Mark did not do much running as most of his time was taken up playing football. He did however win his school cross country race and admits that he should probably have represented Lancashire as a schoolboy, but tended not to turn up for important races as he was happy playing football.

At the age of sixteen, Mark joined the Royal Marines and was thrown into a physically and mentally hard world: 'so even though I wasn't racing I was doing all the ground work, endurance running, circuits and more gym work than I care to remember'. In his first four years in the Marines, work got in the way of racing: the Falklands War, three-month tours of Norway training for mountain and Arctic warfare, working on the raiding and landing craft, a tour of Northern Ireland and an eight-month tour on HMS *Fearless*. The last thing he wanted to do was run . . . what he wanted to do was the same as every other marine: 'go ashore and get down to the pub'.

On joining 45 Commando in Arbroath he was asked to join the Royal Marines Biathlon Team. 'For me this was the chance of a lifetime. I was about to be paid to do sport, and I was going to make the most of every opportunity and I believe I did!' Within a year he was in the national team and over the next 7 years represented Great Britain twenty-two times at World Cup level, thirty-one times in other internationals, at two World Championships and one Olympic Games, in Albertville, France.

He then decided to hang up his skis and give fell running, which he had started as training for skiing, a serious go. He won his first ever fell race and over the years racked up plenty more victo-

ries, not only on the trails and fells, but also cross country and mountain running and more recently on the roads as well, including:

- 1993 British and English fell running champion;
- represented England six times at the World Trophy and once at the European Trophy;
- won the international Knockdu and Snowdon races;
- won the Yorkshire 3 Peaks Race in 1999;
- represented Britain at the 1994 World Half Marathon and has a pb of 1hr 3min 47sec;
- selected to represent Great Britain in the 1995 Marathon World Cup, and has a pb of 2hrs 16mins 03sec;
- won National and Northern 12-stage road relay titles;
- won three Lancashire cross country titles and finished as high as 7th in the National, where he has also twice been member of the winning Bingley team;
- represented the North and England at cross country.

Mark's Top Tips
- Try and have some routine, so you can build up training slowly, enabling you to gain a good base and also avoid injury. Once you have this you should have no problem in doing good quality work and races.
- Running must fit into your lifestyle and your lifestyle must fit into your running.
- Train on all types of surfaces as this will give you all-round strength and the ability to adapt. It can also give you a needed change from the same old routes.

Typical Training
A week's training prior to winning an England World Trophy Trial Race:

	am	pm
Monday	9 mile road	5 mile fells
Tuesday	8 mile road	1hr 15min (club run working hard on the hills round Lancaster)
Wednesday	12 mile road	5 mile fells
Thursday	8 mile road	track 8 × 400m, 8 × 200m
Friday	5 mile fells	
Saturday	10 mile road	
Sunday	1hr 30min fells	

IF YOU WANT TO KNOW MORE

Trail Running Association (which has associate member status of UK Athletics), 141 Davies Road, Nottingham, NG2 5HZ.

The Association publishes a newsletter called *The Trailrunner*, as well as two race directories: The Endurance Directory which contains races longer than a half marathon (both on road and trail and is published in association with the Road Runners Club) and a Short Trail Fixture List, both of which are free to members. It has also produced *A Guide to Organising Trail Races*.

CHAPTER SIX
Cross Country

WHAT IS CROSS COUNTRY?

Cross country is probably the form of off-road running competition with which runners are likely to be the most familiar, if only in its incarnation as a form of punishment or use in bad weather while at school. While it may no longer be an Olympic event, it is the most mainstream of the off-road disciplines and has the most high profile. (Orienteering is the only one of the disciplines covered in this book that has its own national and international governing organization and is run as a totally separate sport, not as a branch of athletics.)

Cross country refers really just to racing and competition, rather than simply running in the countryside. That is not to say that many runners do not run across country while training, it is just that this activity now tends to be called trail or just off-road running.

COMPETITION

Structure

If you want to compete, racing cross country offers something for everyone. At the top end of the sport the annual World Cross Country Championships caters for an abundance of elite middle and long distance talent. In 1998, the Championships changed from one race each for men and women, to a short race (4km) and a long race (8km for women; 12km for men) for each, as well as junior races (U20 in the calendar year). The argument in favour of this change is that it gives more athletes an opportunity to compete over the country at a distance similar to that of their summer track and road outings. In reality, while it has both added extra interest and diluted the title of World Champion, the 'long' races are still the ones to win.

At the opposite end of the spectrum, and seemingly light years away from the televised, sponsored, World and European Championships are the local league events. For many, the leagues are the life-blood of the sport, and a typical afternoon of racing will find hundreds of runners, male and female, fast and not so fast, old and young, competing in a series of races. There are more than fifty British cross country leagues, most based on geographical lines, although there are exceptions such as the university and forces leagues. The West Yorkshire League, for example, has four events each season, held from October to January, with each event hosting races for different age groups. There are no prizes for winning individual races, although overall league winners are awarded medals. While different leagues and championships have recommended race distances, these will vary both between types of event and at races within a league series.

All standards of runner are catered for in league races, and it is common to see international cross country specialists, good club runners, international fell runners and orienteers, track runners, plus plenty of 'every-day'

Typical Cross Country League Race Structure	
Age Group	Approximate Distance
U13 girls	3km
U13 boys	3.5–4km
U15 girls	3.5–4km
U15 boys	4–4.5km
U17 girls	4–4.5km
U17 boys	5–6.0km
U20 women	5–6.0km
U20 men	5–6.0km
senior and veteran women	5–6.0km
senior and veteran men	9–10.0km

The Cross Country Season	
Race	Time of Year
Local leagues	October–March
National Reebok league (including European Championship trial)	October–December
European Championships	December
County Championships (club teams)	early January
Area Championships (club teams)	late January
Inter-County Championships	early February
National Championships (club teams)	late February
World Championships	early March

ordinary runners all using the same race for different purposes. For some, this may be their key goal of the year, or that part of the season; for others the races make a useful hard training run.

If the local leagues and the World Championships are the opposite ends of the cross country spectrum, then there are plenty of races in-between, meaning that whatever level your ability you can find a suitable race to compete in. While the national and international cross country calendar is forever changing, the approximate dates of certain races are given in the box. In addition, there are various international cross country races, and numerous local 'open' races throughout the year. Finally there are cross country relays which take place throughout the season, some more serious and formal (national championships and so on) than other traditional club-based fixtures.

Practicalities

Runners of more mature years reminisce frequently of the days when cross country races where just that – run over real country (mud, ploughed fields, rough grass, without paths), with real obstacles (streams, fallen trees, hills, steep descents, woods and twisty rutted sections) to negotiate. Although 'real' cross country is still found, at the top end of the sport more often than not the courses have a closer resemblance to a track race on grass, albeit one with a few artificial hillocks to go over or logs to jump.

While most runners would probably happily accept the above generalizations as true, there are always exceptions. Here the weather, more than the race organizer, plays a critical part. Excessive rain can turn everything other than the most immaculately drained grass into a quagmire. Nowhere was this better illustrated than the 1999 European Championships, when torrential rain meant that the purpose-built course did not have time to settle and bed down. Most of the newly laid topsoil was washed away and the organizers had to effect a hasty repair by putting considerable amounts of sand onto the course. This leads nicely to the most important rule of successful cross country racing: 'be prepared for anything', especially if the race is being held at a venue with which you are not familiar.

Given the type of terrain required, plus the logistics of hundreds of runners competing in different races held throughout the day, cross country races frequently use schools or other

Real cross country.

community buildings to host the event. Whereas in fell and trail races you can often get away with turning up with minimum time before the start (just enough time to register), doing so before a cross country race is not so wise.

On arrival you will need to:

- find your number: most events require pre-registration, with team managers collecting all the numbers for their clubs' runners;
- find the changing room and the toilets;
- get to the course: this can often be up to a mile away;
- check the route for your particular race: most events use a main loop with add-ons and short cuts, the actual route each race takes, and the number of loops run will differ, depending on the distance;

- decide what to wear, particularly on your feet.

It is wise to leave enough time to either walk round the course or jog round as part of your pre-race warm up, making sure that you keep out of the way of those racing before you. This serves a number of purposes, not least ensuring that you know where you will be going during the race. It can also be useful to find any tricky or narrow points on the course, so that not only do you know what to expect in the race, but you can also work out your tactics accordingly.

For example, if you know there is a fallen tree to either jump or go round at a certain point on the course you will be prepared for it, even if during the race you do not actually see the log until the last moment due to the other runners around you. Suddenly seeing the log for the first time as those in front of you go over or round it is likely to result in you losing time or, at worst, falling over it. With pre-knowledge you may be able to use the obstacle to your advantage and potentially gain places. Alternatively, there may be a narrow gap on the course. If you are part of a big group as you approach the gap, you can either accelerate to reach it in front of those around you, or be prepared to lose time when slowing down to let others through first.

Finally, going round the course beforehand will help you decide what to wear on your feet and, in particular, what length spikes to use. You might find that while the course does have some seriously muddy bits on it, it also includes a stretch of tarmac. This will discussed in more detail later.

At the very least, it is worth looking at both the start and the finish of the course. To ensure that all teams are able to have at least one runner on the start line, the start of a cross country race is much wider than for road or other races of a similarly sized field. This width does not, however, last long and the course will soon become narrow. Starts of cross country races are typically fast and furious affairs as runners sprint to get a good position. It is therefore worth checking out the first 600m of the course so you know what to expect and can plan accordingly. For example, if the course remains wide for some time, then you might be better off starting slightly slower and working your way though the field more gradually. On tighter courses, this will not be such an attractive option.

The finish, like all races, is the scene of flat-out sprinting as runners try one last time to overtake those around them. Cross country race finishes are perhaps more intense than most, as runners fight for team points based on race position. At many cross country races it is not just the first three teams that matter, with the results providing a complete list of teams. Again, it is worth checking out what the run-in to the finish is like (uphill, downhill, the length of the straight, and so on), as well as where the best conditions underfoot will be found, so that you can plan your tactics accordingly.

As most events cater for all ages, there is usually a series of races at staggered times. Often the younger age groups race first and the seniors last. Theoretically, each race should start at the allotted time. While there may be delays at some events, the major ones tend to run to time, even if this means starting one race before all the runners in the previous race have finished, so keeping an eye on the clock is important. Being caught half ready when the gun goes off is not conducive to a good race. Most organizers sound a warning signal at a predetermined time before the start of each race (five, three and one minute are all often used). At this point, runners are required to line up behind the start line, where marshals will normally allocate teams to starting positions or pens. In major races actual pens are often used, with all runners from the same team in one pen, with the faster runners at the front. If pens are not provided, most cross country races will still require teams to line up in the order determined by the organizers.

Once you finish the race you may be handed a small token showing your position. This is not for you to keep, rather it is to be given to your team manager. Although many races now have computerized results, the token system, whereby each team manager collects the tokens from the team members and works out the team's cumulative scores is often still used as a backup.

One last thing to remember, especially for senior runners, is that if the course is wet, by the time you race the conditions underfoot may be very different to when you originally walked or jogged around, having been churned up by the previous age group races.

Start of a cross country race.

CLOTHING AND EQUIPMENT

When thinking about what kit you need for a cross country race, it is worth being prepared for all eventualities. If you are travelling on a team bus, the day is likely to involve quite a bit of hanging around either before or after your race, or both. Given the time of year, there is also a good chance that the place where you will be waiting will be cold, wet and muddy. The last thing you want to happen pre-race is to get cold, so that you have to spend your warm-up time concentrating on getting feeling back into your fingers and toes, rather than on the race itself. So, make sure that you take enough warm and dry kit to see you through:

- standing around beforehand (wellies and a coat?);
- walking/jogging the course and warming up (trainers and waterproof running jacket?);
- racing (spikes and vest, maybe a thermal top?);
- warming down (trainers and waterproof running jacket?);
- standing around, chatting (wellies and a coat?).

Also think about other clothing, for example how many pairs of socks will you need to ensure that you have a dry pair for the journey home – two? three?

Making sure you are warm enough when actually racing is also critical if you are to perform to your best. If your body temperature is below optimal and you spend the whole time trying just to generate body heat, this is likely to have an adverse effect on your performance. It is surprising how many runners (particularly in the younger age groups) are unprepared for the conditions, racing in just vest and shorts when it is near freezing, wet, and windy. This amount of clothing might be fine if you are running fast and generating enough heat to keep warm, but further down the field are those running slower and getting colder. Here, there is the potential for a vicious circle to start:

Running slower and wearing limited clothing;
→ not generating much heat;
→ becoming cold;
→ slowing down;
→ generating even less heat; and so on.

The current fashion for women to wear crop tops in the cold seems bizarre and makes no physiological sense, even if combined with a hat.

What you wear on your feet in cross country can have a considerable impact on the result. Depending upon the nature of the course, cross country races can (and have been) successfully completed barefoot, in

Kit List to Take to a Cross Country Race
Running spikes
Range of different length spikes
Vaseline
Spanner and spike key
Duct or insulation tape
Two or three pairs of socks
Trainers
Wellies or walking boots
Shorts and vest
Thermal tops – one or two
Leggings or tracksuit – one or two pairs
Waterproof jacket and trousers
Warmer jacket
Hat
Gloves
Food and drink (possibly hot?) for before and after the race
Toilet roll
Large black plastic bag (useful to sit on, stretch on, put kit in etc.)
Umbrella
Fleece top

racing flats and trail-type shoes. For most occasions, however, running spikes are more appropriate. Studded fell or orienteering shoes are a very viable alternative, especially if large parts of the course are on tarmac or packed gravel, it is frozen hard or just not too muddy. For those who compete on the fells or similar and already own a pair of fell shoes, using them in cross country races means avoiding the expense of buying another pair of shoes you might only wear three or four times a year. Heavier runners, and those who require a little more motion support, are also likely to find that fell shoes, while not as cushioned or as stable as road ones, are likely to be better than spikes.

If you are reasonably serious about competing cross country, it is worth investing in a pair of spiked shoes. Not only are they lighter and more responsive than fell shoes, but due to the spikes in the sole, they are normally better at coping with the conditions underfoot. With spiked shoes there are two things to consider: the shoes and the spikes.

Considering the shoe itself, there are a couple of things that need to be taken into account when deciding what to buy. Firstly do you chose a primarily track-based spiked shoe, which will be lighter, more flexible, and more responsive but also more flimsy or alternatively, one designed specifically for cross country? The latter will probably have some form of studs or waffle heel to enhance grip as well as a more substantive, protective upper, and potentially more motion support for the foot. The downside is that these shoes will also tend to be slightly heavier and not as flexible. There are pros and cons to both types of shoe. Most top class cross country runners go for distance-based track spikes. However, considered as a group they will be running faster (less heel-ground contact) and will have better mechanics than the average runner and will often be running on 'tame' man-made courses. For those who may be heavier,

slower or not so biomechanically efficient a more supportive shoe with additional heel grip might be better.

The other thing to consider about the shoe itself is the amount of heel lift or wedge. Runners susceptible to Achilles tendon-related problems should opt for a shoe with a greater wedge or lift.

Buying the shoes themselves is not enough: next come the actual spikes. Most shoes will come with a set of spikes but, especially if you are buying by mail order, do not take it for granted that they will be the length that you want. If you are taking cross country at all seriously, you will need to equip yourself with a selection of spike lengths, as well as accompanying paraphernalia.

The length of spikes to chose depends partly on personal preference, but mainly on what the course is like underfoot. For dry, good-going courses, 9mm spikes will probably be sufficient (9mm is the length of the actual spike, not including the part that screws into the shoe). For muddy, rougher, ground, 12mm spikes are preferable, while 15mm might be needed for really bad conditions. An alternative to wearing spikes all of the same size might be to use three 12mm spikes in the holes nearer the back of the shoe, with three 9mm spikes towards the front.

Do not think, however, that longer is always better. Spikes that are too long will not only act more as a braking force but also increase the potential for tripping, as well as injury due to excessive strain on the soft tissues around the ankle.

Most runners will take a selection of spikes with them to a race, along with:

- spike key (a special tool to remove and tighten spikes);
- pliers or spanner, for loosening stubborn or rusty spikes;
- Vaseline (not only useful to rub on your legs if very cold, but also if smeared onto

the spikes before inserting into the shoe will make for easier removal later);

- lubricating oil (this can also be used to make spike removal easier, but is not suitable for spraying on your legs);
- duct tape (some runners, particularly junior ones, wrap duct tape around their shoes to help keep them on their feet, especially if the course is very muddy).

Ideally, you should remove your spikes from the shoes after each race. In practice, most runners do not do this, changing spikes only when different length spikes are needed or the original ones have worn down. This increases the likelihood of finding that one or more spikes have become stuck. In a worst case scenario, this can mean a spike that can not be replaced or damage to the spike unit when trying to remove it. To minimize this risk, it is advisable to put a little oil or Vaseline on the spike before inserting it into the shoe. The night before a race, check both that you can undo the spikes and also that they are firmly tightened and have not come loose.

TRAINING

Training for cross country racing is essentially no different to that for any other similar length event, be it on the road or track. The same principles apply. As with other off-road disciplines, the terrain needs to be taken into consideration. Road and track runners planning on racing cross country would be well advised to do some of their speed or effort sessions (ideally one per week) on undulating grass surfaces. Particularly in wet muddy conditions this will mean that you are running slower than for the equivalent time or distance on good surfaces, but the effort should be the same and it will help build the additional leg strength needed for cross country.

One particular aspect of cross country which is worth specifically working on in training is the ability to achieve a fast start before settling down into a steady rhythm without 'dying'. You have to be able to cope with working anaerobically for a short (2 to 3min) period of time before easing into a more aerobic mode. This is followed at the end of the race by a sustained or shorter flat-out drive to the finish. Put another way, your body has to be able to cope with an initial increase in circulating blood lactate, one that can then be dissipated (recovery) while still running at a sustained racing pace, before repeating the process of running fast at the end of the race when you are tired. One of the best ways of preparing for this is to replicate it in training, for example, on grass running:

- 15 to 20min sustained, with a hard first 3min;
- 3min fast; 1min recovery; 10 to 15min sustained; 1min recovery; 2min flat out;
- 3 × 1min hard; 15min sustained; 3 × 1min hard; all off 1min recovery.

While doing some sessions on race-like terrain is useful, it is also worth keeping some speed work on 'faster' surfaces such as good trails, or grass, track or road. This will help maintain and increase your underlying speed. Remember, especially for women, cross country races may be less than 20min in length, so speed as well as strength–endurance will be important.

NUTRITION

The major point regarding nutrition and cross country is to be prepared; even better, be self-sufficient. Competing in league and other structured events often means an early start and a long day, especially if you travel on the team bus which has to reach the event in plenty of time for the first race and will not leave until after the last. It is important to make sure that you have all you need in terms of energy and fluid for both your pre- and

Runner Biography

Angela Mudge must be the nearest thing to the complete off-road runner: World Mountain Running Champion, British and Scottish fell running champion, Intercounties and Scottish cross country champion, as well as winner of numerous mountain marathons. Why no notable performances yet on the roads? That is easy to answer: she does not like them as much as the hills.

As a child, Angela did lots of sport, but was not very co-ordinated so ended up taking a shine to cycling, swimming and running: 'Anything without a bat and ball'. With her family, she also spent a lot of time tramping around the local hills.

Angela started running whilst at senior school, 'but was too slow to do the sprints and got shoved in the 1500m as a first year'. She competed for Devon as a junior, going to English Schools track and field champs (3000m), and cross country ('finishing 206th as a 13 year old'). When she was 16, a local father spotted her and twin sister, Janice, and started coaching them.

Once at university she tried and liked orienteering. From Leicester University, she moved to Stirling to study for an MSc and fell in love with the hills. She joined the Ochil Hill Runners and was hooked. Her first fell race was Carnethy 5, which ended in tears as she spent the next four months away from serious running with Achilles tendonitis. Angela then moved to Edinburgh University, from where she graduated in 2000 with a PhD entitled 'Mass Spectrometric Characterisation of Priority Pollutants'. This, she notes, is 'not an interesting topic, a cross between analytical chemistry and instrument development'.

Whilst at Edinburgh, she started training properly and over the next few years progressed from just scraping into the Scottish mountain running team, to being picked automatically – the hard work paid off. Angela notes that the improvement was mostly due to putting some structure into her training and getting away from lots of long slow running, which she loves, to more productive and painful speed work.

While studying for her PhD, she was able to find time to race in Europe in some of the grand prix races. As of 2001, Angela's work career has been put on hold for a few years whilst she spends summers in the Alps to concentrate on running. Despite receiving Lottery funding from **sports**cotland, Angela tries to pick jobs up at home to get some cash and through the winter save her from the boredom of being a full-time athlete: 'I need something other than athletics to focus on day in and day out'.

While mainly a mountain and fell runner, Angela's successes are wider and include:

- 1st 1999 Intercounties and Scottish cross country championships;
- 1999 World cross country championships, 45th;
- World mountain running trophy six times, including 1st in 2000;
- European mountain running trophy five times, including 2nd in 1999 and 2001;
- British fell running champion 1996–2000;
- winner of European mountain running grand prix in 1999 and 2000; and
- winner of elite KIMM with Helen Diamantides.

Despite all of the successes listed above, Angela rates her best performance to date as winning Sierre Zinal in 2001 in a new record and becoming the first woman to break 3 hours. (The previous record had been set in 1987 by V. Marot, who went on to run 2.25 for the marathon. For more on the importance of Sierre Zinal, *see* the profile of Billy Burns in Chapter 8.)

continued overleaf

Angela Mudge

Angela winning the Yorkshire 3 Peaks Fell Race.

Runner Biography: Angela Mudge *continued*

Angela's Top Tips

- Use your training and racing to explore new places. Most weekends I'm off training somewhere different.
- Set realistic goals – there is nothing worse than finishing every race disappointed.
- Don't get stuck in a rut. I aim to do one or two new long races a year (and a few short ones). Don't go back to the same old races year in year out, try something new.
- Enjoy it – why else do it?
- Use your mates for training, I have my easy running crowd and my 'hang on for dear life' crowd.
- If you are going out in the hills for a long run don't forget the jelly babies! And learn to navigate.

Typical Training

Monday	up to 1hr easy	pm circuits
Tuesday	am 30–40min	pm track session i.e. 5 × 1000m or 6 × 800m
Wednesday	am 50–60min steady	pm circuits
Thursday	am 30–40min easy	pm hills or longer reps
Friday	40min easy	
Saturday	race or tempo run or long day in the hills	
Sunday	long run in hills >2hr, or long trail run in town <2hr, or a mega day in the hills, Angela will often miss a Sunday run for a long day in the hills, 'great way to build stamina'.	

When preparing for the cross country season, Angela's training follows a fairly standard pattern (above). This is mainly used as a way to keep fit for the summer, as she needs something to aim for to keep motivated to train hard. Angela also loves racing and cross country is the best surface in the winter.

During the summer Angela heads for the Alps for 2 to 3 months, taking her touring bike and tent. A hint for those thinking of trying it, take something bigger than a Jetpacker! The races are spread around in Italy, Austria, Switzerland, Germany and Slovenia, so Angela cycles around local areas and catches the train for longer journeys. She tends to base herself in one valley for a week (normally the week leading up to a race) and uses her running to explore the valley. She does not have a typical week's training as it is dependent on what the area has to offer. 'I love the St Moritz valley for its lakes or the Wallis area for its glaciers. I'm not fussy as long as there are beautiful hills and views about. As long as I am getting to explore new areas and running new races I could go on for years.'

Angela often trains first thing in the morning and then spends the rest of the day walking in the area, taking her butties with her in her bumbag. On days where she does hard sessions, it is more about finding somewhere nice to enjoy the recovery.

post-race needs. Do not just rely on motorway service stations and the whim of the bus driver to stop. Doing this might mean that before the event you either leave too long between eating and racing, or that the time is too short: in either scenario you will not run as well as possible. After the race, not eating within the first couple of hours (and particularly the first 30min), or not eating enough or the 'wrong' things after racing, will delay your recovery, potentially adversely affecting your training over the next couple of days.

CHAPTER SEVEN

Fell Running

WHAT IS FELL RUNNING?

The Collins English dictionary defines fell as 'a mountain, hill or tract of upland moor'. Fell running is therefore running over such terrain. By its very nature, pure fell running is about being in countryside that is mainly unspoilt, exposed, wild, beautiful and also often potentially dangerous. It is about running without paths and restrictions or encountering hordes of people in the hills. People chose to run on the fells not only for the challenge that it brings but also because of the environment within which it takes place.

The two key points to remember when fell running are, first, to be sensible and make sure that you know enough about what you are doing to minimize any potential risks and, secondly, to respect the countryside in which you are running and those that look after it. Respect for the countryside was discussed in Chapter 5, to which for those planning to venture off trail and onto fell, the following points are worth adding:

- Make sure that you are aware of any other events taking place where you plan to run. In many parts of Scotland and the North of England, stalking and shooting are major businesses and runners should avoid these areas as appropriate.
- Avoiding livestock means all animals, especially young ones. Deer calves, etc. should be admired from afar and certainly not touched, as a young animal which smells of humans may be abandoned by its mother.
- Much of fell running takes place off paths. However, where you are following a marked path try to stick to it and not run just to one side. This might be easier or drier for you but it will also increase erosion. Likewise, where paths have been strengthened or upgraded, for example on many of the popular Lakeland, Snowdonia and Pennine routes, stick to them and do not cut corners. This is important even if it would be easier to run on the grass rather than on the flagstones themselves, especially when they are wet and slippery.

Safety

A major part of why people run on the fells is the freedom, the environment and a love of remote and less inhabited places. With this comes an increased potential for difficulties. This should not be a problem if you are sensible.

Many fell runners get immeasurable pleasure from running on the fells without ever going near a race. For those looking for suitable long distance challenges not involving pinning a number to their chest, the fells can provide plenty of opportunities. Over the years, a number of circular or point-to-point routes taking in a series of summits have been developed. Perhaps the most well known of these is the Bob Graham Round in the Lakes. Named after its instigator, the BGR (as it is known) involves forty-two Lake District fell

---

Be Safe on the Hills

- Think about the weather, not just where you are and now, but what is forecast and what this will mean where you are planning to go. Temperatures, wind and rain in the valley will not be so pleasant at a height of 500m or more. Make sure that you are prepared for the worst. This does not mean it is necessary to overdress: it is common to see fell runners in shorts and thermal top running past walkers in full body waterproofs, gaiters, rucksacks and even carrying ice axes. If you are moving fast (a skill in itself), you will keep warm and carrying a lightweight waterproof, plus hat and gloves, is often sufficient.
- Most of what you carry is not to wear unless you have an accident. If you twist an ankle or worse and have to slow down, you will chill off very quickly. If you are at all unsure about your ability to run over the terrain, you should take a spare layer with you. This is best kept in a plastic bag to keep it dry, inside a bumbag or small rucksack.
- For the same reason take a whistle to call for help if needed. Alternatively, you may consider carrying a mobile phone, but bear in mind that in more remote areas it may not be possible to obtain a good signal.

- Unless in familiar surroundings, take a map (either waterproofed or in a plastic map case) and make sure that you, or one of your companions, know how to read it. A compass is also usually worth taking.
- Wear appropriate footwear.
- Do you need to take some food? Fluids may or may not be such a problem, depending on the availability of streams.
- There may also be specific local hazards to beware. In certain parts of Scotland ticks, particularly from deer, can be a major problem, giving hours of post-run entertainment either searching your own, or someone else's uncovered parts for them. To remove a tick, you can cover the tick in Vaseline, or something similar, which will suffocate it, causing it to fall off. Alternatively, use a pair of sharp pointed tweezers to firmly pull the tick out with an anticlockwise movement (make sure you get the mouth part), after which you should use antiseptic on the bite area. Make sure that the head is removed, because if it is left behind the potential for infection will be increased. This can cause Lyme's disease, which, while rare, can have irreversible effects similar to arthritis or rheumatism.

---

tops, approximately 72 miles and 27,000ft of climbing. To qualify as a member of the BGR 24-hour club the round has to be completed within 24 hours, either clockwise or anticlockwise, starting and finishing at Keswick Moot Hall. Other popular rounds include the Ramsey Round (Scotland) and the Paddy Buckley Round (Wales).

For some runners there is nothing better than making up their own route, either covering a certain number of peaks, Munros (Scottish mountains over 3,000ft) and so on or linking places together, either in celebration of a significant birthday, or 'just because'.

COMPETITIONS

Structure

Fell racing is a pretty unique British tradition and it is only in this country that you will come across 'true' fell races, as opposed to long trail or mountain races, although there is often considerable crossover. What makes a fell race a fell race? Like trail races, fell races come in many different guises. Races run under the auspices of the Fell Runners Association (FRA), the governing body of the sport in the UK, are covered by the FRA's insurance policy.

Traditionally, a fell race could be described as a relatively low key event (in comparison to many road races), which involves visiting a series of checkpoints, or a single checkpoint, on the fell, including one or more climbs and descents, running on open terrain. More often than not the checkpoints are on summits, with many race routes following classic lines defined by geography, for example Grisedale, Peris or Kentmere, which are horseshoe-shaped courses run on ridges. Variables include whether the route is marked, how much route choice is involved, the severity of the climbs and descents and the terrain underfoot.

Some of this race information can be obtained from the annual FRA Fixtures Calendar and Handbook, sent at the beginning of the year to all members of the Association. This, however, does not include the majority of Scottish races and many Welsh ones, as separate fixture lists for these are produced by the Scottish and Welsh respectively, available from the addresses given at the end of this chapter.

All races in the FRA handbook are classified in two ways, by length and by 'difficulty'. Three race lengths are used:

- L (long): 12 miles or over;
- M (medium): 6 miles and over but under 12;
- S (short): under 6 miles.

Classifications are:

- 'A' races should average not less than 250ft of climb per mile, be at least 1 mile in length and have less than 20 per cent of the race distance on road.
- 'B' races should average not less than 125ft of climb per mile and have no more than 30 per cent of the distance on road.
- 'C' races should average not less than 100ft of climb per mile, contain some genuine fell terrain and have not more than 40 per cent of the distance on road.

Every race is therefore defined by two letters,

with C category races being the easiest, often not much harder than many trail races. A races, particularly long ones, are at the other end of the spectrum and should not be tackled without thought and without experience of other fell races. Many race entries also note whether the course is partially marked, whether navigational skills are required, if local knowledge is an advantage or whether experience is required. Some races, for example the 3 Peaks or Ben Nevis, require evidence of experience in other similar races before accepting your entry.

For the extra competitive there are annual British and home country (England, Scotland, Northern Ireland and Wales) Championships. For senior and veteran runners each championship currently involves the best scores from up to four of six designated races, including at least one of each distance (S, M, and L). The championship races are selected each year, with those from the British Championships including at least one from each of the four home countries. There are also English championships for junior runners at U12, U14, U16 and U20.

Internationally, home country teams compete in a number of events as listed in the calendar. The European and World Trophy events, although coming under the auspices of fell running, will be covered in Chapter 8 (mountain running).

Just to confuse matters there is also the British Open Fell Runners Association (BOFRA), which has its own circuit of races, which are traditionally short and steep. Historically BOFRA or open races (also previously called guides races) were professional races which gave money as prizes. Amateur runners were not allowed to compete in BOFRA races without consequently being banned from other forms of running, in line with the then amateur ethos of athletics generally. It is only relatively recently, now the sport is open, that runners can compete in both series of races without problems and

Grisedale Horseshoe race.

repercussions. BOFRA have their own calendar of races and championship series.

Practicalities

Given the possible range of conditions, unless you know the race well, it is always worth going prepared. The FRA rules states that race organizers should require runners to carry the following:

- windproof full body cover;
- other body cover appropriate for the weather conditions;
- map and compass suitable for navigating the course;
- whistle;
- emergency food (long races only).

The safety requirements, which form part of the FRA race insurance cover, say that organizers should check the above by holding kit checks. Organizers are allowed to waive some or all of the requirements if the weather is fine. In practice, this means that some races (typically C, shorter, ones) very rarely require runners to carry anything although they might, however, recommend it. Others (normally long 'harder' races) will require compulsory kit to be carried.

When deciding what to take to a race, it is always better to be prepared. Remember the very nature of most fell races means that they are held in exposed places where the conditions are likely to be more severe than when you set off from home for the race.

Many fell races, particularly those in the Lakes and Scotland, involve unmarked, off path, courses requiring route choice between checkpoints. This leaves the runner with a number of alternatives, the least attractive of which is just following the rest of the field and hoping in the mist that those you are following do not go wrong. Trying to follow runners from local clubs is usually a better option, but certainly not foolproof. Some runners also take delight in deliberately leading astray runners who are blatantly following them. A more sensible alternative is to combine the former with making use of your map and compass as you go along. Most runners will do some pre-race homework in preparing their map by marking on checkpoints (using indelible ink), and working out best lines to and off controls and noting bearings to follow.

For those local enough, or who can spend some time beforehand, some pre-race reconnaissance should ensure you work out the best line to take, as well as identify some familiar landmarks to check off during the race. However, make sure that you stick to rights of way and footpaths. Quite a few races, for example Stanbury and the 3 Peaks, obtain special permission from landowners to take the race over private land. Recceing the route in these cases may jeopardize the future of the race.

When choosing the best line to take it is worth remembering that what is best for one runner may not be the best for you, in terms of terrain underfoot and your ability to move fast over it. While some runners might prefer and be better (faster) over a short rocky scramble with no paths, others will opt for a longer route involving fast running on paths.

CLOTHING AND EQUIPMENT

For runners deciding to take up fell running, shoes aside, there is little additional kit needed. When both racing and training, being well prepared is not being 'soft'; rather, it is not being stupid.

Socks

Your feet will inevitably get wet. There are various options available for those who suffer from cold feet (trying to run with numb feet is not pleasant). Wool socks are popular, with other choices being Poreal Drys, Gore-Tex or neoprene socks. Using Gore-Tex or neoprene socks may mean a bigger shoe size as the socks can be quite bulky.

Wind/Waterproofs

Many races require you to carry full body cover. It is worthwhile investing in a lightweight Pertex or similar top and bottoms. Alternatively, rip-stop nylon (like a tent outer) will keep you warmer and dryer, but is not breathable. For more severe weather, a lightweight Gore-Tex top or similar is useful (and like the other options, can easily be fitted into a bumbag).

Hat/Balaclava

Around 30 per cent of heat loss is from the head, and thus some form of appropriate head gear in the cold therefore makes sense. Waterproof hats or balaclavas are often used, but make sure that your choice is close fitting and will not blow off in the wind. It also often makes sense to wear lightweight head cover in the summer, especially in longer events, to help avoid heat-related headaches, sunstroke etc.

Gloves

When thinking about gloves, remember that you are likely to have to use your hands when fell running, either to use the map/compass or when tackling steep, rocky ascents and descents. You may also be left with wet hands. You may therefore want to consider gloves made from wind or rainproof material. While these are likely to be more expensive, they will help keep your hands functioning.

Base Layers

Thermal or technical tops are pretty essential for all year round use. Use multiple thin layers rather than fewer thicker ones as this allows for better temperature control linked to height climbed/wind/rain and exposure. Leggings and/or mid-thigh tights are also useful, but make sure they do not become baggy when wet or muddy.

Bumbag

If you are going to race or run on the fells regularly you will need a bumbag. Traditionalists tend to go for the bare essentials: either a top with a pocket that can turn into a bumbag or a simple bumbag with compression straps. More sophisticated, bigger versions with thicker material, bottle holders and different zips tend to be heavier and more expensive. If it is wet or hot remember to put the bumbag contents into a plastic bag to protect them from rain or sweat.

Shoes

Shoes are probably the most important item of kit and if you are going to run or race regularly on the fells, a pair of shoes designed for the purpose will be a wise investment. For a variety of reasons ordinary trainers or those designed for trail running will function less than optimally on most fell terrain. In particular they will be lacking in grip, too wide, with too much heel depth (and therefore unstable).

A number of the major running shoe companies have at times produced fell shoes. At the time of writing Nike, New Balance and Reebok have all discontinued their ranges, while Adidas' is going strong. There are currently two specialist companies that make fell shoes: the Felldancer and Walsh ranges. Both these have been designed specifically for British fell running. What, then, makes a good fell shoe?

- **Grip.** Deep, moulded studs (fell shoes are often known as studs) are best.
- **Rubber.** The ability of a fell shoe to 'stick' to rock (and not slip, especially when foot contact is not on flat rock), both wet and dry is important and will depend on the rubber compound used to make the sole. Unfortunately softer rubbers, which tend to stick better, also tend to be less durable.
- **Fit.** The snugger the fit, the better, in order to prevent excessive movement of

the foot in the shoe. The type of ground you will be running over often means continuous changes of foot plant position on uneven, frequently sloping ground. The potential for friction (and blisters) between sock/shoe and foot is considerable. For some runners even using fell shoes does not prevent blisters, but zinc oxide tape or something similar over the vulnerable areas often does the trick.

- **Upper.** This needs to be: robust, to prevent tearing or ripping and give some protection; flexible and lightweight, to help ensure a snug fit; quick drying; semi-waterproof; and breathable, so as not to hold water. Do not expect a rigid shell-like upper on a fell shoe.

- **Profile, or depth.** This does not refer to how the shoe fits around the foot, rather how the foot interacts with the ground. Fell shoes only have a thin mid-sole and typically one which is flat from heel to toe (not sloping as for road trainers). This creates a very low profile, flat but stable, foot position. The downside of this is that it is often difficult to put orthotics (inserts to help control abnormal foot movement) into fell shoes.

Where fell routes are primarily over grass or mud (not rocky terrain) orienteering shoes, which have small spikes on the studs, or fell shoes with spikes are also often used.

TRAINING

If you are going to be successful at fell running, just being fast and having good endurance, while an advantage, will not be enough. You need to be able to transfer these attributes into the environment in which you will be competing. That, for fell running, means two things.

First, being able to cope and run fast over the underfoot terrain (*see* Chapter 3). The second key transfer needed concerns hills, and the ability to get both up and down them quickly. As well as doing specific hill reps in training, long days out in the fells mixing walking and running are good forms of preparation, and will help condition your legs (and arms) for both ascending and descending. The very nature of the terrain, in that it is soft underfoot and that you are going to be mixing walking and running means that 4 to 5hr-plus efforts on the fells are probably not much harder (if at all) than 2hr on reasonably flat trails or roads. In fact, you are very likely (quadriceps aside) to feel less sore and stiff afterwards.

Kit to Take to a Fell Race

Shoes. Depending on the course take fell shoes plus training/racing flats. Some races will always be best done in studs, others if dry are often better tackled in flats (for example Skiddaw, Hutton Roof or Pen y Ghent).

Shorts and vest.

Socks – may be different types depending on the conditions.

Long and mid-thigh tights (be prepared to race in these, especially during the winter).

Short and long sleeved thermal top.

Lightweight windproof full body cover, including hat and gloves.

Thicker waterproofs, if bad weather is likely.

Bumbag.

Whistle and compass.

Food (if long race), plus something to eat afterwards.

Map – carrying a complete Harvey's or Ordnance Survey map is bulky, the alternative is to cut a map down. This can then be laminated, with the checkpoints marked on it in indelible ink.

This type of long day out, as well as being enjoyable:

- Helps your descending, the less breaking and more flowing action you can develop, the less muscle damage. Also, the more descending you do, the more your quadriceps muscles become conditioned and therefore less liable to soreness in the first place (specificity of training).
- Lets you practise running in terrain.
- Improves your ability to walk fast up long hills. In A and B category fell races all but the very top runners will either walk the climbs or mix walking and running. With certain climbs (Ben Nevis for example), everybody walks at some point. Being able to walk efficiently and fast is therefore a must. Most people use a low style, using their hands to push off from the quadriceps muscle just above the knee. Good walkers are often faster uphill than those who prefer to try and run the whole climb. Bouts of walking also have the advantage of using slightly different muscle groups, therefore allowing the muscles used in running some recovery.

The other form of training that is excellent for climbing is cycling and there are numerous examples of athletes who compete at a high level both on the fells and the bike and of runners who do much of their training on the bike (see Chapter 8).

You may well find that your post-event recovery times are different when racing on the fells compared to the roads. Events involving long, sustained, fast descents (such as Skiddaw and Wrekin) are notorious for post-race muscle soreness. This may last for up to a week, during which time you are probably better off avoiding running, and sticking to alternatives such as swimming or cycling. Trying to run too soon, as well as being acutely painful, can have long-term consequences. The soreness and stiffness is

likely to inhibit your normal running style, making you run in an 'adapted' way, which in turn can lead to other injuries.

Long fell races (2hr plus), on the other hand, require less recovery time than races of comparable time or distance on the roads. This is because both intensity of effort and patterns of movement tend to be more variable during a fell race. While you will experience the same feelings of tiredness on finishing, as well as short-term stiffness, the longer term recovery process, until you are back in full training, is likely to take less time.

NUTRITION

Probably the biggest consideration for fell runners is drinking. In longer races, eating is also an issue, but this is easily solved by carrying your personal choice of carbohydrate with you in your bumbag. If possible, take something which you have practised eating while on training runs and are comfortable with. It may seem obvious, but eating on the uphill sections, especially on long 'walking climbs', is much easier than trying to do so when either running fast downhill or involved in negotiating tricky underfoot terrain.

Assuming that, for most fell races, any official drinks stations are few and far between, if in existence, what do you do? Well there are a number of options:

- Drink nothing: not so clever in 4hr-plus races.
- Carry it with you, either in a bottle, a hand carrier or Lucozade pouch or similar.
- Arrange for friends to meet you at set points on the course with drinks.
- Drink from streams when you can. This is usually safe in the higher fells, but a bit more suspect nearer civilization (remember to check that a dead sheep is not in the water just round the corner). Always try to drink from fast running water and not stagnant ponds. One tip used by a lot of runners is to carry small waterproof plastic bags contain-

Runner Biography: Ian Holmes

If you go to one of the four fell races organized annually from Howarth, it is a good bet that it will be won by Ian Holmes. In the ten years to 2001, he had only been beaten in these races three times, and one of those was when he fell badly and had to retire. He has won the Stoop race 10 years in a row, and is the only ever winner of the Auld Lang Syne race, and it is not for the want of trying by other top runners.

It is not just in local races however that Ian comes out on top. He is one of the best fell runners in the country, and is also pretty handy on the road, cross country, in mountain races and the occasional mountain marathon.

As a child, his first love was rugby (as an early developer for a while his 5ft 9in frame was an advantage). Having had to give rugby up due to a bad back, he came under the wing of another top Bingley fell runner, Ian Ferguson. Ian the older used to take a group of younger lads off at weekends climbing, caving and fell running. This Ian admits: 'was something to do before going to the pub'.

While working as a ski instructor/guide in Italy, Ian started to train more seriously. Not giving any consideration to the altitude (5,500ft) he trained twice a day, more importantly experimenting with what he did, including doing a hard session every day for ten days in a row. He also read Ron Hill's books: 'which made me realise what hard training really is'.

On returning to England, Ian and wife-to-be Zena settled in Keighley, where he now works as a whirlpool fitter. More importantly he started racing seriously on the fells, gaining his first England vest at the 1992 World Trophy, where he came 28th. Since then Ian has:

- been British fell running champion five times, and English Champion three times;
- represented England in the World Trophy four times, as well as at the European Trophy and all the other major international events;
- won most of the classic fell races, including Ben Nevis (four times), Burnsall, 3 Peaks, Jura, Borrowdale, Snowdon and Langdale;
- become a household name in Indonesia by winning the Mount Kinabalu race three times in succession;
- won gold medals at the National 12 stage, National 6 stage, Northern and Yorkshire road relays;
- finished 50th in the National cross country, 9th in the Northerns and 4th in the Yorshires (picking up either gold or silver team medals in each).

On the fells Ian is renowned for his descending ability, noting that when he is fit he feels he can beat anyone. It is not unusual in a straight up and down race (such as Ben Nevis) for him to be some distance behind the first runners to the top, only to easily catch them on the way down. To him it makes sense, seeing it as an opportunity to get away from the opposition without having to put in as much effort as would be needed if trying to do the same while running uphill.

Ian's Top Tips

- Set goals for your running, but be patient.
- Train for the event you are aiming for: if you want to run fast on the fells, train on the fells, not just round a track.
- Join a good running club, one that has a good social side as well. If you want to be a successful runner a large proportion of your time will be spent either running or with runners.
- Try to recce fell races beforehand.
- Have some sort of race plan before you start, but be prepared to change it depending on what happens and other runners do. *continued overleaf*

Ian winning Ben Nevis.

Typical Training

Eight years ago Ian used to train up to twelve times per week, running to and from work, with at least a couple of quality sessions each week. Now family commitments mean he trains slightly less, up to ten sessions in a good week, and he admits that he often misses one or two sessions a week.

Monday to Friday   three 30min morning runs
   four 40–50min evening runs
   one 20min sustained run
Saturday   50min run
Sunday   90min run

Ian does not do any additional strength work, but he has a physical job. Despite being one of, if not the best, descender in the country, he never runs hard downhill in training. Ian always makes sure that he is fresh for races, easing down beforehand more than he used to and always taking the day before a race off.

Ian stressed the importance of preparing mentally as well as physically for races. For a couple of weeks before a major race he starts thinking about it, noting that: 'however fit you are if you are going to win or do your best you have to be prepared for it to hurt'. He works out a race plan, based on the route and who else is competing. For example, with some top runners Ian knows that he can let them get ahead of him on a climb because he will catch them on the downhill.

ing some energy powder. These can then be filled at streams and drunk using a bendy straw (also carried). If you are worried about the quality of the water, iodine or other sterilization tablets should be used.

● Go out the day before and hide drinks near road crossings or on the course. You will need to remember which rock you hid your drink behind and also hope that none of the faster runners has already 'borrowed' it.

Whichever method you use, always remember not to just throw your empty drinks container away – take it with you or hand it back to a friend or a spectator.

IF YOU WANT TO KNOW MORE

The Fell Runners Association, 34A Kirkland, Kendal, LA9 5AD Tel: 01539 731012. Membership includes an annual calendar and the *Fellrunner* magazine three times a year. Fell Runners Association website: www. fellrunner.org.uk

Scottish Hill Runners website: www. hillrunning.com

Welsh Fellrunners, 11 Pen y Graig Terrace, Pontypool, NP4 5JS. Tel: 01495 758141.

N. Ireland Fellrunners Association website: www.nifra.org.uk

BOFRA, 53 Westburn Cresent, Keighley, West Yorkshire

N. Matthews and D. Quinlan, *Fell and Hill Running* (UK Athletics, 1996)

CHAPTER EIGHT
Mountain Running

WHAT IS MOUNTAIN RUNNING?

In its simplest form, mountain running is running in the mountains, normally on good trails and paths. Mountain racing is a predominantly continental sport, involving running up mountains, normally on a mixture of road and good off-road trails with no navigation or route choice required. A few races are all tarmac, while Pikes Peak is a fine example of an American mountain race. While Italy has a number of mountain races involving both ascent and descent, most other continental races are uphill, or predominantly uphill, only.

Mountain running and mountain racing as it is on the continent does not really occur in Great Britain. The reason for this is simple: Britain does not much suitable topology or underfoot terrain (or the weather) for mountain races. While there are plenty of mountains, particularly in Scotland, they are smaller – the highest, Ben Nevis, is 'only' 1,344m, compared to the frequent 3,000m, let along 4,000m peaks in Europe. British mountains are also not so accessible in terms of roads or tracks on which the events can take place. Finally there is the difference in underfoot conditions and weather: wet peat bog and heather, compared to alpine type passes and meadows. The nearest race to a mountain race in Britain would probably be Snowdon, and that is up and down.

Running in the mountains can be a pleasure in itself and many British runners make annual summer trips to the Alps, Pyrenees or further afield to enjoy running and racing in (usually) good weather and stunning surroundings. Here the relevant safety points given in Chapters 5 and 7 should be followed. One of the advantages of many mountain paths is that that they can be accessed by cable car networks. These can be used either to reduce the time spent getting up high or to avoid the need to run back down again (and suffer the associated muscle damage and soreness).

Mountain paths are usually well marked, either by signs or coloured markings painted onto rocks (a little more difficult to find in winter). You are encouraged to stick to the official path, both for your own personal safety, either from wildlife or the terrain, and from an environmental perspective. For those looking for longer multi-day trips in the mountains, some countries require you to purchase a permit to camp in the various campsites on the trails, and you are not allowed to camp elsewhere.

As with British footpaths and rights of way, all mountain paths are not the same. Those used for races and the main paths tend to be well defined and pretty good underfoot. As long as you have a reasonable head for heights, you should be fine. Other paths can mean a mix of running, walking and scrambling, although most of the popular routes tend to have protection in the form of wire ropes to hold on to for narrow ledges or where there are particularly steep drops. For the more adventurous type, wanting more than just straight running, challenges such as the Via Ferrata in the Dolomites (making use of wire ropes, ladders and rungs for the tricky bits) are available.

For those planning to embark on this type of trip, a bit of research before you set off is well worthwhile. In particular, make use of the relevant tourist office to get the best travel and accommodation deals. This can mean as much as half-price travel on trains, buses and cable cars. It is also worth finding out whether there are any local restrictions that might affect your plans. In some countries, paths can be closed due to adverse weather or the presence of wild animals such as bears close by.

COMPETITIONS

Mountain racing is a well established and very competitive form of running in Europe. The major races are significant local and even national events, with invited elite runners, prize money, long prize lists and usually both pre- and post-race entertainment. Most races are uphill only, or include only limited amounts of descending. Typically, a race will start in a town centre and follow a series of roads and good tracks uphill to the finish. This is either located near the top of a cable car (Matterhornlauf) or at a village further up the valley (Sierre-Zinal).

At the elite end of the sport are runners capable of breaking 64 and 71min (men and women respectively) for a half marathon on the roads. However, mountain running in Europe is enjoyed by all levels of runner and while at the front it is serious, the races normally have a very festive and relaxed atmosphere. One race in Switzerland turns the drinks stations into wine stations for the runners to stop off at on their way back down the mountain once they have finished. At some events there is a tourist category, where the participants, either walking or jogging,

set off earlier than the faster runners in the main race.

The mountain race season runs from May to October or November. For those wanting race details, then the *Berglauf Journal* is probably your first port of call. This annual German language publication is more than just a directory of around 100 races in Germany, Italy, Switzerland, France and Austria. It also provides a review of the previous season, course profiles and descriptions, profiles of star runners, as well as training advice. The Swiss also produce an annual guide to races, including mountain ones. Race lengths vary and while there are some longer ones, most tend to be around 8 to 20km long and winning times will obviously be longer than for the same distance on the road. The 8km Grabs race for example climbs nearly 1,000m and takes the men's winner around 45min. Ovronnaz-Cabane Rambert, also 8km, but with 1,300m of climbing, takes the men's winner more than one hour.

Most races will have drinks stations, and in some of the longer races, food as well, although these will be located where possible rather than at set kilometre markers. You should expect to pay more for your race entry than in Britain, but this will normally cover your transport back from the finish to the start of the race.

For elite runners there are the World and European Mountain Running Trophies. These are held in July and September respectively and alternate between an uphill only and an up and down course. One year the World trophy will be uphill only and the Europeans up and down, and vice versa the following year. This arrangement is a compromise between those countries who traditionally prefer up and down races and those who favour uphill only ones.

There are also two mountain running grand prix race series which runners take part in as individuals, as opposed to the national teams that compete in the European and

World events. The World Mountain Running Association runs a six-race grand prix, the races in which change each year. More traditional is the Berglauf grand prix series consisting of six of the most well-known mountain running events. In both series the individual races carry prize money, as well as overall series prize money.

While prize money might be beyond the realms of most runners, alpine races are renowned for their extensive prize lists covering all the age groups for both men and women. Typically these are much more generous than the prizes found at British races. The prizes are donated by the local community and shops; for example hotel accommodation, cheeses, wine and local goods.

You may also come across reference to a much more extreme (and therefore potentially dangerous) form of mountain racing called Sky Racing. These races are probably best left alone by all but the fittest and most experienced runners. The conditions under which the events take place are severe in terms of terrain, weather and altitude, and often with minimal safety precautions.

CLOTHING AND EQUIPMENT

For those simply wanting to explore the various mountain paths and tracks, then the safety kit guidelines given in Chapter 7 should be taken into account. Remember that although the weather might at first seem warm and sunny, in most mountainous regions it can rapidly change to cold, windy and wet.

Footwear will be very important for those interested in mountain racing. Traditional British-style fell shoes are fairly unique to this country, although they are becoming more popular on the continent. The surface for most mountain races in Europe is typically packed earth trails, paths or roads in various states of repair. This means that in most cases normal road racing flats or light trainers are

suitable to wear while racing. It can however be worth taking trail or fell-type shoes with you 'just in case'. A sudden downpour can turn a course into a muddy quagmire, in which case better grip will be invaluable, especially if the course includes any descending.

Ski or trekking poles are becoming increasingly common in mountain races, as well as for use by those out in the mountains. While these may not be used by the super-fit elite, for those runners further back in the pack they can be useful:

- to reduce the pressure or load on your knees: it has been estimated that that 5 to 28 per cent of body weight can be transferred onto the poles (the higher figure when using two poles and in difficult, descending terrain);
- for climbing (when walking or slow running) they can help provide additional leverage in the same way that ski poles do for the cross-country skier;
- on the flat, if the ground is very rough underfoot, poles can help maintain balance by increasing the number of points of contact with the ground from one (your foot) to two or three (depending on how many poles you have);
- for descending they can again help balance and stability, this time acting in a similar manner to an alpine skier's poles.

However, trekking poles are not permitted in all races.

TRAINING

In terms of 'intensity' profile most mountain races have more in common with road races than ones on the fells. Mountain, like road racing, requires a constant, sustained effort, except it is travelling primarily uphill rather than on the flat. You will not experience the

European Trophy 1996: note the road racing flats.

changes in intensity which are found in fell races due to alterations in conditions underfoot or topology.

This therefore needs to be taken into account when training. Sustained runs on the flat or over hilly courses are beneficial, and will provide an appropriate stimulus to the cardiovascular system. They do not however replicate the demands placed on the leg musculature, in particular the quadriceps and hamstrings. The ability to carry out long sustained uphill runs on relatively good surfaces is limited in Britain. Even mountains like Snowdon or Skiddaw will give you only around 8km of uphill running, and unless you are on Snowdon where you can catch a train, you will then have to run or walk back down again, potentially either becoming cold, suffering from eccentric muscle damage, or both.

The alternative to spending periods training in the Alps or other such areas is to incorporate more cycling into your training. Perhaps the ultimate training programme, and one used successfully by many international mountain runners, is to incorporate both running and cycling uphill in the mountains. The demand on the muscles when running uphill is similar to that required for cycling. If your race plans involve considerable amounts of uphill running (either on the fells or mountain racing) then incorporating some cycling into your training programme is certainly worth considering.

There are, however, a number of pluses and minuses associated with this. On the plus side cycling is non-impact (as long as you do not crash) and therefore puts less stress on the joints. It is also, however, generally accepted that the performance benefits of cycling on the flat compared to running are not a straight 1:1 swap (one hour's cycling is not equivalent to one hour's running). It takes longer cycling compared to running to get the same performance benefit, except when cycling uphill. Many of the top competitors will interchange sessions such as 30min sustained work as either running or uphill cycling.

Especially in the winter, it is not always easy to cycle on the roads with any degree of safety or comfort. One possibility is to use a turbo trainer, which converts your road or mountain bike into an indoor stationary one. Depending on the make, the turbo either fits around the back wheel of the bike or attaches to both the front and back. Rollers, on the other hand, are a set of rollers onto which you balance your bike. These require better bike handling skills but promote a smoother pedalling action.

How then is it best to fit cycling into your training programme? The aim should be to substitute some of your running sessions with sessions on the bike designed to have similar physiological training effects. Adding one or

	Sunday	Monday	Tuesday	Wednesday	Thursday	Friday	Saturday
running	long run up to 2hr	steady run	intervals	medium length run	hills	rest	off-road hilly fartlek
running and cycling	alternate weeks long run (90–120min) or ride (2–4hr)	steady run	intervals	steady ride can you cycle to and from work?	bike intervals on turbo	rest	off-road hilly fartlek

Including Cycling in Your Training Schedule

In the winter it might be easier to switch the Wednesday ride to Saturday.

Bike Training Tips

- Make sure that your bike is correctly set up for you in order to prevent overuse injuries (all good bike shops should help you with this).
- Unless doing hill reps keep the revs (how fast your legs go round) high, aiming for 80–90+ revs per minute.
- Long endurance runs can be replaced by 2 to 4hr bike rides.
- Riding uphill and out of the saddle makes the mechanical action more specific to uphill running.
- If using a heart rate monitor, your heart rate is likely to be slightly lower than running both for steady state training and harder intervals when on the bike (this is due to the smaller muscle mass being used).
- Do hill sessions on the bike, here the revs will be lower.

- Get on the turbo/bike straight after a long run. This not only increases the time during which you are training with minimal added impact, but does so in a mountain running friendly fashion.
- If you have access to a turbo, very specific, controlled sessions that replicate those you would do running can easily be done for example:

  - 30min sustained, high pedal revs
  - 10: 8: 6: 4: 2: minutes, 1min recovery
  - 5–10 × 5 minutes, 1min recovery

- Similar sessions can obviously be done on the road, but it is more difficult to control the session in terms of traffic, road signals and topology and so on.

---

two cycling sessions a week is also a possibility for runners wanting to increase their overall amount of training, but worried about the injury risk associated with increased running mileage. Not only does it provide a slightly different training stimulus, but does so without increasing the impact stress on the joints.

Altitude

The other key point that needs to be considered when thinking about mountain running, and in particular mountain racing, is altitude. Many of the races not only finish but also start at altitude. It is important to plan your travel details and timings to ensure that you do not to reach the start line at the wrong point in your body's adaptation process. If you get it wrong, both your race experience (how much you enjoy it and how good you feel during the race) and your race performance (how well you do) are likely to be adversely affected. In addition, the consequence of trying to run hard at the wrong time can leave you feeling too unwell to enjoy

the post-event celebrations.

Altitude refers to the vertical height above sea level. As altitude increases the air pressure decreases. This means that, while the concentration of oxygen in the air (just under 21 per cent) is the same, the partial pressure of the oxygen is reduced. Why is this important? Oxygen transfer across the surface of the lungs occurs because there is a difference in the oxygen partial pressure between the lungs (high) and the blood (lower). This difference in pressure facilitates the movement of oxygen across the surface of the lungs. As you go to higher altitudes the pressure difference decreases, and as a result the haemoglobin (the oxygen carrier in the blood) is not completely saturated with oxygen, as it is at sea level.

While, to a degree, a lower atmospheric pressure (and therefore lower air resistance) will aid sprinting performances, it will adversely affect endurance performance due to the decrease in the amount of oxygen available to support performance. At lower levels of altitude you may not notice this effect while just walking around. However, at altitudes of over approximately 1,500m, running endurance events will start to be adversely affected (above 1,600m $\dot{V}O_2$max decreases by 11 per cent for every 1,000m increase).

When you first arrive at a higher altitude your body starts to go through a period of adaptation to try to acclimatize to the new environmental conditions.

- Breathing rate increases to bring in a larger volume of air and therefore oxygen. One side effect of this is a reduction in the blood's ability to buffer acidic conditions (and therefore a reduced tolerance to lactic acid).
- Blood volume decreases over the first few weeks at altitude. As the number of red blood cells stay the same, this helps increase the amount of oxygen that can be delivered per volume of blood. With time at altitude the blood volume returns to normal. However, the number of red blood cells then increases, which results in the blood volume increasing above its normal level.
- Maximum heart rate and stroke volume decrease.
- At sub-maximal workloads the body relies more than usual on anaerobic energy production with resultant higher levels of lactate. At maximal work rates, lactate levels are lower.

While the adverse affects of altitude mean that running endurance performances are unlikely to ever match those at sea level, acclimatization does help reduce the decrease in performance. However, the physiological adaptations take time, and typically the higher the altitude the longer acclimatization takes. For altitudes of between 1,500 to 2,000m, a minimum of 2 weeks, but preferably 4 to 6 weeks, should be allowed for full acclimatization.

While 2 weeks acclimatizing prior to competing may be possible for some, for most recreational runners it will be unrealistic. What is important is to optimize the time of arrival at altitude prior to the race to minimize the detrimental effect. There are two options for this:

- Arrive within 24 hours of the race start. This will mean that while you will be affected by the altitude you will not be adversely affected by the subsequent physiological changes that take place as your body starts to acclimatize.
- Leave at least 6 or 7 days between arrival and competing. Your physical work capacity is reduced during the first few days at altitude. Anecdotal, rather than scientific, evidence suggests days 4 to 6 (depending on the individual) are the 'worst' for trying to race.

There are a few other things worth taking into account when planning a trip or run at altitude:

- Temperature drops approximately 1°C for every 150m climbed so you should take appropriate kit with you.
- The air at altitude tends to be 'drier' or less humid. This increases sweat and insensible water loss meaning dehydration is more likely. Ensure that you drink more than normal and remember the urine test.
- The thinner and drier air means solar radiation is greater, so use appropriate sun protection.

Training at Altitude

- Only train easily on the first 2 or 3 days.
- As heart rates will be lower, use subjective feeling to gauge training run intensity.
- If doing interval type training, increase the recovery period between efforts.

Runner Biography: Billy Burns

In certain parts of Europe, Billy Burns is a star and a household name, to be feted when ever he turns up at a race. This is not due to having run a 2.15hr marathon and represented England at the Commonwealth Games, but because he has won what for many is the biggest race there is on the summer mountain running circuit: Sierre Zinal.

Like many children, Billy played football as a youngster, taking up running at the relatively late age of twenty when he decided to try something different. He saw a 10km race advertised in the local paper, and with 2 weeks' notice decided to enter it. Two weeks' hard training later he finished in 33.31, coming 9th, feeling disappointed. Luckily for Billy, who admits that at this stage he 'had no knowledge about what he should do', he began chatting to the race winner (in 31min) who encouraged him, telling him that he could become an international runner, but that it would take 5 years.

Billy started fell racing in 1993, coming 2nd in his first race. Here he was leading until the last section of the descent when the fact that he was wearing road shoes proved to be a slight disadvantage. Two races later, and wearing fell shoes, he won his first fell race. More importantly: 'I had found something I really enjoyed, winning or not'.

In 1997 Billy took time out to spend the summer racing in Switzerland. With fellow runner Matt Moorhouse he cycle-toured between races and lived in a tent for 2 months. 'This was a fantastic experience, cycling up the cols (mountain passes) and training in spectacular scenery', which also got Billy very fit. 'I loved it and still do.' Billy returned to the mountains each of the next four summers, and as he improved so he has won most of the classic mountain races: Thyon-Dixence; the Matterhornlauf; and of course the real classic of the Swiss Alps, Sierre Zinal. Unless you have been there it is a little difficult to visualize what this race means to the local population. Running 31km from Sierre in the valley up to Zinal (with 2,000m of climbing and nearly 1,000m descending), it draws massive crowds and provides instant fame for its winners.

In between his summer trips to the Alps, Billy decided in February 1998 to train for that year's London marathon. Before this, the furthest he had raced on the roads was 10 miles. Three days later and he was flying to Kenya for 2 months' training. Here everything was perfect: climate, diet, training and the added benefits of altitude, all of which resulted in a 2.15 clocking and selection for the 1998 Commonwealth Games.

Other than the track, Billy has represented England on all surfaces; road, cross country, fell and mountain running, including:

- Mountain running World Trophy four times, finishing 3rd in 2001;
- Mountain running European Trophy;
- Commonwealth Games marathon in 1998;
- His road pbs include 29.31 for 10km and 2.15.40 for the marathon.

Billy's Top Tips

- Plan your training and learn how to time it so that you train hard and rest in the correct periods depending on what events are important for you. For example, I like to be at my lowest fitness in December and June, and be in peak form in April (spring marathon) and September (World Mountain Running Trophy).
- Make use of cross training. When you are struggling to get out of the door (for whatever reason, injury, bad weather, lack of enthusiasm), it is good to try something different at home. I have various pieces of exercise equipment, giving me as many options as possible to prevent me from getting bored. These include making use of road and mountain bikes, turbo trainer, cross-country ski

continued overleaf

Billy qualifying for another England mountain running team.

machine, in-line skates, and aqua running. If you do not want to buy the various pieces of equipment then join a gym that has a good range of aerobic machines.

● Make the most of your environment. I change my environment to Kenya and Switzerland but a lot of people are not even aware of what is in their local area. I always try to explore different places – get an Ordnance Survey map and you'll find lots of different footpaths you have ran past not knowing they existed. The long Sunday run is the best time to go exploring.

Typical Training

This was the last hard week's training carried out by Billy in St Moritz in 2001 before easing down for a week prior to the World Trophy.

Monday	am 45min easy	pm 25min warm up 45min threshold
Tuesday	am 30min warm up; 4 × 3,000m, 2min recovery; 20min warm down	pm rest
Wednesday	am 45min easy	pm 20min warm up; 30min threshold; 20min warm down
Thursday	am 30min warm up; 40–60min hard uphill only 20min down (this session can be done on the bike)	pm 30min easy
Friday	am 30min warm up; 25 × 400m, 1min recovery; 20min easy	pm rest
Saturday	long walk (this session would either be a 2hr slow run, a long walk or 6hr cycle, on this occasion Billy walked as his foot was sore)	
Sun	rest	

NUTRITION

Nutrition for mountain running is no different from other endurance events. If you are interested in long days out in the mountains, then the points covered in the chapters on fell and mountain marathons will be relevant. For those looking to race in the mountains, then a normal endurance runner's diet is important.

There are however three provisos for both groups if at altitude:

● Be aware of dehydration and make an effort to drink more.

● You are likely to use more glycogen in training during your first few days at altitude, make sure therefore that you eat accordingly.

● Sufficient iron-containing foods should be eaten to support the increased red blood cell production.

IF YOU WANT TO KNOW MORE

Raatz, W. *Berglauf Journal* (w-u-s-media, annual publication)
Websites: www.berglaufgrandprix.com; www.wmra.info

CHAPTER NINE
Orienteering

WHAT IS ORIENTEERING?

Orienteering has been described as 'finding your way through a forest using a map and a compass', others may prefer the description 'like doing *The Times* crossword while running for a train'. As a sport it is both and more. Orienteering can be a competitive test of physiological endurance, technical ability and concentration, or it can be a fun day out for all the family.

Orienteering involves locating a series of predetermined checkpoints, usually in wooded or open moorland terrain, navigating using a map and compass. For the competitive, it is about doing so as fast as possible, for many others it is a personal challenge where good route choice, accurate navigation and having an enjoyable day out are more important.

Most orienteering, even for the non-competitive, takes place at events, if only for access to pre-placed controls and their associated maps and description sheets. There are also numerous permanent orienteering courses around the country in easy to access parks and woodland. These courses have a series of permanent wooden controls, and maps of the area with the controls marked on are available, usually from local council or tourist offices. As well as a good place to start orienteering, they can also provide a useful training environment for other runners who need to be able to use a map and compass. The fact that there are permanent controls means there should be no doubt when you

are in the right place – assuming, of course, that the control has not been vandalized. A list of the permanent courses in Britain can be obtained from the sport's national governing body, the British Orienteering Federation (BOF).

As a sport, the concept of orienteering has also been adapted for, amongst others, canoeing, mountain biking, skiing, diving and those whose mobility is impaired (trail O). For runners there are also score events (where you have to gather as many points as possible in an allotted time, with each control having a certain number of points), night orienteering (in the dark using a head torch) and street orienteering (in urban areas).

Orienteering is renowned as a family sport. The different level courses mean there is something for all abilities and ages. String courses are laid for the very young. These are about 1km in length and marked with string or tape to follow, often using pictures on the control cards rather than descriptions.

COMPETITIONS

At first glance finding your way around the variety of orienteering competitions might appear daunting. This is perhaps not helped by the tendency to abbreviate everything (clubs, competitions and events) to initials only. The World Orienteering Championships is therefore known as WOC (pronounced like the cooking implement) and the junior version J WOC (two words).

Colour Coded Events

At the base of the competition structure are local and colour coded events. These are organized by clubs and offer a range of courses for different abilities. Colour coded events have up to ten different colours (or courses). Courses of the same colour at different events should be approximately the same standard and length. The ten colours cover five different levels of technical (orienteering) ability, with the additional colours relating to longer courses at certain levels.

Colour coded events frequently form the basis of local or regional orienteering leagues.

Entry usually takes place on the day. If you wish to compete, you must arrive at the race registration, which is often a car park or similar, and pay an entry fee. You then say which course you want to do and buy a map (which does not have the controls marked on it), a control description card, and a control card. The control description card provides a brief description of the feature where the control is located, for example knoll E side, or re-entrant, and the control card must be punched at each control to verify that you found it. You will also either be given or allowed to choose a start time. Most events

Description of the Possible Different Courses at a Colour Coded Event		
Colour	Approx. distance and time	Description
white, level 1	1.0–1.5km; 15–35min	very easy, all on paths, no route choice, used mostly by six to ten year olds and family groups
yellow, level 2	1.5–2.5km; 25–45min	easy, route on obvious features such as tracks, paths, walls, no route choice, mostly used by under twelves, families and mobility impaired
orange, level 3, short	2.5–3.5km; 35–60min	moderately easy, some route choice and basic use of compass, mostly used by under fourteens and adult beginners
red, level 3, long	3.5–7.5km; 45–90min	as for orange but with longer distances between controls, mostly used by adult beginners wanting a longer run
light green, level 4	2.5–3.5km; 35–60min	more difficult than orange, going into terrain, offering challenging navigation and route choice, mostly used by under sixteens and adult improvers
green, level 5, short	3.5–5.0km; 45–75min	as difficult as the area will allow, using contour features etc, used mostly by experienced under eighteens and adults wanting a short but challenging course
blue, level 5, medium	5.0–7.5km; 55–90min	as for green but longer and more physically demanding
brown, level 5, long	7.5–10.0km; 65–105min	as for blue but longer

The lengths quoted may vary, particularly in terrain which is physically either very easy or difficult. Purple and black courses are longer level 3 and 5 courses respectively, but are only rarely used.

send runners off at one minute intervals.

When warming up and preparing for your start time, remember to allow enough time to get to the actual event start, as this can be a short distance away from where you register.

The first thing to do once you start is to mark the checkpoints you need to visit on to your map, copying from a master map. These will be displayed near the start, but make sure that you copy from the correct one for your course. Marking the map is best done with a red pen (take your own), putting a small circle around the control feature, making sure that when doing so you do not obscure any important features nearby.

Next, link the controls with a straight line in the order you need to visit them. As the map is unlikely to be waterproof, take along a clear plastic bag or map-case to protect it from rain and sweat.

Once on the course remember to check that the numbers or letters at each control correspond to those next to the control description given on your description sheet. Controls are marked by a small banner or kite with the orienteering symbol (a square divided into red and white triangles). It is not uncommon, especially in small technical areas, for course organizers to put two controls close together. There is nothing worse than getting all the way round only to find that you have visited the wrong control at one point.

If hand punching is used, you will find a spiked punch at the control. This is used to mark the corresponding box on your control card. It is not possible to cheat by punching more than one box at a control as every punch will have a different alignment of spikes. At the finish you will be required to hand your control card in for checking. Even if you do not complete the course you must always report to the finish, otherwise the organizers will think that you are still out on the course and may send people to look for you.

Badge Events

In badge events, courses are based on age groups. There are separate events for men and women at age groups U10, U12, U14, U16, U18, U20, senior, O35, O40 etc. up to O70. At each of the younger age groups, there are normally two courses available, A and B. The B course is shorter and easier than the A course. For the senior plus classes there is usually the option of a short or a long course.

At badge events the technical difficulty of the course will increase as the age group gets older, up to the senior class. After that, as the age group increases the technical level stays approximately the same but the length of the courses decrease. For badge events you usually have to pre-enter (often via e-mail) and you are then provided with a map with the controls pre-printed on and given a start time.

National Events

Above badge events are national events. This is a series of six to eight events held throughout the country. They are slightly longer and are held in good quality (in other words, more technically demanding) terrain with a high standard of mapping. For those so minded the BOF operate a ranking list based on performances at badge and national events, with more points available at national events.

National and International Championships

Finally, for the serious orienteers there are the national championships and for a very few, international events. Orienteering holds its WOC every year, with World Cup races held earlier in the season. At the WOC there are races over sprint (10–15min), short (approximately 25min) and classic (approximately 90min for men and 70min for

Runner arriving at an orienteering control.

women) distances as well as three-runner relays for both men and women.

CLOTHING AND EQUIPMENT

If you want to try orienteering, you can do so with minimal outlay, just a compass, whistle, plastic bag for your map, and red pen (for colour coded events). If you decide to become more serious about the sport, then, while orienteering is not an expensive sport, there are specialist items available to tempt you.

Shoes

Although it is possible to orienteer in ordinary training shoes (especially on the easier courses), either fell shoes or specialist orienteering shoes are more suitable. The latter are like fell shoes in that they are tight fitting, sit close to the ground and have a studded sole. They differ in being more rigid and less flexible, and have a more protective waterproof upper, thus providing more support and protection for your feet. Many orienteers wear shoes with permanent small metal spikes, or dobs, in the studs. These help provide grip in particularly muddy forest undergrowth as well as being surprisingly good on wet rock. Finally, most orienteers wrap a small amount of Duct or insulation tape around the bow of their shoelaces to prevent it either being pulled undone or snagging.

Full Leg and Torso Cover

Orienteering regulations require full leg and torso cover (short sleeved tops are allowed). This means that your legs must be fully covered at all times to prevent scratches and infections. Some countries, Scandinavia in particular, are very strict about this, to the extent of requiring any holes or tears in the trousers (not uncommon) to be taped up. For those starting out, Lycra tights or trackster-style bottoms are fine. You can buy specialist orienteering trousers made of lightweight nylon, which are loose fitting and are certainly more comfortable and cooler in the summer. Tops of the same material, designed for orienteering, are also available. Again, these have the advantage of providing full body cover, but are lightweight, which is particularly good for summer use. Another

Off-road footwear. Clockwise from the top: cross country spikes, fell shoes (studs), orienteering shoes and trail shoes.

alternative preferred by some orienteers is to wear long shorts to below the knee combined with 'bramble basher' socks held up by gaiters, thus preventing any exposure of bare flesh.

Shin Protection/Socks

It only takes one venture onto good quality orienteering terrain at anything other than a slow walking pace to show why some form of leg protection is required and why many orienteers have interesting collections of scars and grazes on their legs. As well as protective footwear and long trousers many orienteers, especially on more technical (that is, thicker undergrowth) courses, will wear additional shin cover. Soccer-style shin pads are one option, particularly for training where the added weight and bulk are offset by the increased protection. More favoured alternatives, especially for racing, are orienteering gaiters, or 'bramble basher' socks, which are padded over the front of the shin.

Eye Protection

It is not uncommon, particularly in Scandinavian countries where there is a large amount of pine-type forest, for orienteers to wear clear glasses to protect their eyes from being caught by a passing branch. The downside is the possibility of the glasses steaming up, bouncing around or catching sweat.

Waterproofs

Waterproofs may be required to be carried if the weather is bad.

Compass

Top orienteers often use the compass as more of a general directional tool, with most of the navigation being done by comparing the features on the map with the land. One of the winners at the 2001 Orienteering World Championships did not use a compass at all.

Many orienteers use a thumb compass rather than a traditional base-plate one (*see* Chapter 4). These are worn on the thumb,

normally the hand in which you hold the map, therefore making 'thumbing' the map easier. As the compass is just used for orientation purposes, many thumb compasses do not have degrees marked on them, just coloured blocks on the housing. The experienced orienteer saves time by not taking a bearing, using the compass instead to set general direction and using the map for finer navigation and feature location.

Due to the very fine, detailed nature of some orienteering maps, especially in Scandinavian countries, many elite and non-elite orienteers also use a magnifying glass. These attach to the compass, magnifying the area of the map underneath, making features easier to distinguish, particularly when running at speed.

Control Card or Electronic Punch

In many events, the system of runners using control cards to register finding a control has been replaced by electronic punches. There are a number of different models on the market, but the principle is the same. Each competitor carries an electronic tag with which they make contact with the housing on the control. This registers that the person has visited that control and the time of their arrival. Organizers are able to track runners centrally, as well as provide detailed time splits at the end of the event. If using electronic punches make sure that you are confident of how they work and that during the event each control registers your punch (this is usually shown by a small flashing light, noise or both). Electronic tags can either be bought or hired at events. As most of the events in Britain use the Sport Ident system, many orienteers buy their own tag.

Map

These are usually either 1:15,000 or 1:10,000 in scale, which is more detailed than the normal OS maps, which are either 1:50,000 or 1:25,000. Maps for events are provided by the organizers. Those used to 'normal' OS maps need to beware as orienteering maps use slightly different colours and symbols. The most obvious example of this being that orienteering maps distinguish between different types of forest. Runnable forest is shaded white, with darker shapes of green used to show increasing thickness. On the other hand, on OS maps all forest/trees are green.

TRAINING

Training for orienteering is not just about getting better at running fast, or even better at doing so for a period of time though seemingly impenetrable woodland. That is only part of it: just as, if not more, important are navigational and route choice ability. It is not unusual for the tortoise to beat the hare if it knows exactly where it is going! Training for orienteering therefore needs to include the following, in addition to 'normal' endurance running training as covered in Chapter 3.

It is also important to do at least some of this training in orienteering-style terrain, which is off-road running at its most extreme. Good runners who are not orienteers often find it difficult to keep up with an orienteer

---

Kit and Equipment List for an Orienteering Event
Shoes and full body cover kit
Map-case/plastic bag
Whistle
Duct or insulation tape
Tape for taping ankles if required
Compass
Waterproof top and bumbag
Safety pins and control card attachment
Waterproof red pen (colour coded events)
Magnifying glass (if used)
Insect repellent (for comfort)
Electronic control (if being used)

---

whom they would normally beat in a cross country race, when running in orienteering terrain. This should include trying to do efforts and sustained runs in terrain.

Map Skills

You will need to train to improve your map skills, in other words how to read a map quickly and accurately and choose the best route after weighing up the various alternatives. Here armchair training can be used to good effect. At its most basic, this can simply be studying maps and making sure that you are comfortable with the various symbols and shadings used and know what each means. Other options include:

- **Reading contours.** Practise with the map so that you become quicker and better at being able to glance at the map and build an accurate 3D picture in your head of what the terrain would look like.
- **Interpreting the map.** Study routes on old orienteering maps and work out what you would expect to see as you followed the route. What handrails and attack points would you use (features on the landscape which will help you to correlate your position with the map and to locate the control point: *see* Chapter 4)? Consider how many paces you think you would take between features.
- **Route planning.** Again using old competition maps, select a series of controls and work out the route you would take between each. This is a good exercise to do with others – did you both pick the same route? If not, why not?
- **Route planning under pressure.** Leading on from the previous exercise, pick a course of say six to ten controls and time yourself while you plan your route – can you do it in less than 2min?
- **Map memory.** Study a route on a map for 30sec, close your eyes, how much of the

route can you remember? And repeat or write down? What features do you pass on the way? These types of training exercise can then be made harder by combining them with a running challenge, so you are physically tired while trying to remember things.

These are just some ideas: the bottom line is there is plenty to be gained by spending time in the comfort of your chair studying maps, looking at features, thinking about routes, route choice and what you would see if you were 'on the ground'.

Map Skills in the Field

Map and compass skills will improve with practice, as will your 'feel' for the terrain. Spending time navigating in the hills will do wonders to improve your ability. For those wanting the more technical challenge of orienteering there are various training exercises/ideas that can be used.

While it is possible to train and practise these various skills and exercise on old courses, depending on the type of training session planned, sometimes a better alternative is to use local colour coded events. Here the advantage is you not only have a course to follow on the map, but also actual controls on the ground as well.

Map Reading on the Move
Reading a map while running is not easy, even on good, even surfaces, let alone through forests and off-trails. Practising reading a map while running faster than 'in terrain' race pace on paths or tracks helps improve your ability to look at the map and take in what information you need at a glance. This does not have to be the map of where you are running, any map will do, preferably one with a suitable scale. Another alternative is to run on the pavements after

dark, using the streetlights as you pass under them to read the map.

Practise Techniques Separately
Practise using one orienteering technique at a time. Most navigation involves using a mixture of the different techniques, such as keeping in contact with the map (i.e. matching features on the map with those on the ground around you as you go along), using compass bearings and pacing. Try finding features, or better still doing a local colour coded event, while only using one of the techniques.

Overkill
Overkill is the opposite of the above, navigating using all the techniques at once: compass, map reading, and pacing.

'Traffic Light Orienteering'
This refers to knowing when to run fast with minimal map contact, when to slow down and start paying more attention to your surroundings, and when to concentrate on the fine detail. It is as much about your state of mind as it is actual speed, and conscious decisions to switch between the colours can be practised while training and in races.

Consider again the example used in Chapter 4 to demonstrate handrails and attack points. You know you have to cross a path on the way between the two controls and can therefore run on 'green' (fast, with minimal attention to the map and surrounding features) until you get there. Between the path and the fence corner a little more care and attention to detail is required. Now you run slightly slower, on 'amber', keeping better map contact and noting features on the way. From the fence corner to the re-entrant, careful navigation is needed so as not to overshoot or miss the control. This calls for fine navigation, running or walking on 'red', probably pacing and keeping in close contact with the map.

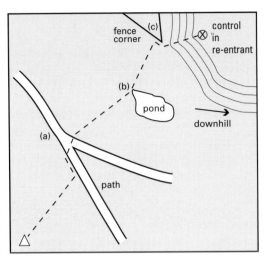

start → a   = on green
a → b → c   = on amber
c → control = on red

Traffic light orienteering.

Relocation Exercises

Relocation exercises help your ability to be able to interpret a map and understand what the features on paper translate to on the ground. The most common is for runners to work in pairs or groups. One person, using a map (the others put theirs away), leads to within say 50 or 100m of a control. The other runners are then allowed to look at their maps, knowing that they are within a certain radius of the marked control. They have to use the ground features to relocate their position on the map and then run to the control. The group then change roles and someone else leads to within 100m of the next control. This exercise can lead to heated discussions if there is disagreement about where the group actually are on the map.

Incomplete Maps

'Incomplete' maps are often used as exercises by orienteering clubs and squads. For these you need maps especially produced for the purpose which are missing certain features. For example, you might have to navigate using a map only with contours on it, nothing else, or one from which all paths and roads have been removed. Another alternative is to block out sections of the map.

Thinking Ahead

It is useful to practise focusing your mind ahead of your body, or as you are running thinking about upcoming features rather than those you have just passed. This way you are thinking ahead rather than behind. As you are running, consciously work to keep your mind in front, expecting and looking for the next feature, rather than taking in those around or behind you. Practising this skill at a colour coded event means that you can start off on a course with a lower technical level if necessary.

Memory Games

Any form of mental/memory challenge combined with a running one will help improve your ability to take in, memorize and use large amounts of information quickly, while also working physically. For example, look at a control description card for 30sec while jogging slowly, then run hard for 2min, stop and see how many of the descriptions you can remember and are they in the right order? Alternatively, design a circuit training session where every other or every third challenge is a mental rather than a physical one.

NUTRITION

The only additional point to make here relates to fluid intake. You are unlikely to find drinks stations provided at local events or during shorter races. On longer courses (over 60min) at larger events there may be drinks stations, but while these will be marked on the map, they might not be on the route you would normally plan to take between two

Runner Biography: Yvette Baker

During the mid-1990s there was one name that female orienteers feared more than any: Yvette Baker (née Hague). Yvette was the most consistent elite orienteer in the World. It did not matter what the terrain was like, either fast running or Nordic and tricky, if she did not win, Yvette invariably would medal. And this in a sport that non-Scandinavians are not meant to be good at (certainly not in Nordic terrain). The summit of this period of dominance was winning the World Championship short course race in 1999. Before this, she had already picked up three other World Championship medals, including silver in both the short and classic races in 1995.

Yvette was introduced to the sport by her parents at the age of seven. By the time she was twelve years old, a mixture of orienteering and athletics training meant she was one of the best for her age in the country. Yvette continued to combine the two – while it was obvious she was better at orienteering, she admits to 'getting a real buzz out of the head to head competition of athletics that you do not get in orienteering'. Unfortunately, when she was sixteen she developed the shin problems which were to plague her for the next thirteen years until successfully operated on in 1996. In the intervening years, it meant that her athletics career was curtailed.

The diagnosis of compartment syndrome (where the restriction of the periosteum sheath round the muscle results in pain during exercise) meant that Yvette had to compromise her training, concentrating on quality not quantity, avoiding running on the roads and doing more cycling.

After leaving school, Yvette took a year out to concentrate on orienteering, working as an au pair in Sweden for six months. While the finances of the sport meant that it was not possible to make a living from orienteering, she wanted to be the best orienteer in the world and made decisions accordingly. This included her career, where early thoughts of becoming an earthquake seismologist went out of the window when she realized that the types of places she would be working were not compatible with orienteering. 'I set my mind on becoming a World Champion while watching the World Champs in Scotland in 1976 (age nine). I saw Liisa Vejalainen (Finland) run up the run in to win and I was so impressed, I wanted to do it too!'

Instead, Yvette read geophysics at Edinburgh University, graduating in 1990, by which time she had already run in four World Championships. In order to concentrate on her sport, Yvette decided to work part-time. In hindsight she now realizes that while she got very fit during this period, her competitive career 'stagnated without something to challenge my mind'. Registering to study for a MSc got her back on track academically and her orienteering results started to pick up as she claimed her first World Championship medal in 1993.

A part-time job as a research assistant, where she was able to work hard in the winter and do very little in the summer, apart from orienteer, led to registering for a PhD in computational geology. Currently living in Denmark where her husband works, she is in the process of finishing her PhD and after the 2001 World Championships announced her retirement from international orienteering. But not running. She loves the feeling of 'flowing easily though terrain and on the hills' too much for that.

As Britain's greatest ever orienteer Yvette:

- represented Great Britain at every World Championships between 1985 and 2001;
- won four World Championship medals, including gold in the short event in Scotland in 1999;
- finished third overall in the World Cup series in 1992 and second in 1994;
- has finished in the 20s in both the National and Intercounties cross country championships;
- represented England at mountain running;
- has won many of the classic fell races such as Langdale, 3 Shires and Borrowdale, here she was often seen with her map out even on marked courses, 'to take my mind off the pain on the long uphill sections!'
- has a 1,500m pb of 4.40, set at the age of fifteen.

Runner Biography: Yvette Baker *continued*

Yvette at the 2001 World Championships, her last international orienteering event.

Despite all of these, Yvette's favourite achievement (apart from becoming World Champion) was winning a World Cup race in Sweden in front of a Channel Four television crew who were making a documentary and wanted to illustrate how good the Swedes were at orienteering.

Yvette's Top Tips

- When orienteering you need to concentrate all the time, you can not afford to let your mind wander. Despite winning the World Championships at the short distance, Yvette considers herself a better classic runner, preferring the longer distance 'as it requires you to be able to concentrate for long periods. The shorter distance races do not test this ability so much. It is relatively easy to hold your concentration for 20 minutes, but 60 minutes plus is much harder'.

- Look at old courses the night before a race to help get your mind into the right frame of mind. This can either be maps from previous races where you did really well or ones where you made a mistake, but this time going through the race in your head you correct it and have a good run.
- Learn to anticipate what to expect. It is the ability to anticipate which skills you are likely to need as well as what might go wrong, which separates the very elite from the good. If you have already anticipated a problem and solved it in your mind, if it does happen in reality it is not such a problem.
- However important your sport is make sure that you have a life as well. It is damaging for you and your sport to make it the 'only thing'.

Typical Training

An example of a typical week's training in the 4-month build up to the 1999 World Championships, when she aimed to do 2 hard weeks of around 60 to 80 miles a week, followed by an easy one at 40 miles. Those thinking that these are 'low' mileages for an elite runner should remember that this was all in terrain, not on roads or track. Races were frequently used for training purposes.

Mon	am 50 min (6 miles) easy terrain run	pm 5 miles slow on grass
Tue	am 12 × 1km on grass (3.35–3.40), 45sec recovery	pm 80 min bike ride on the road
Wed	am rest	pm 11 miles terrain run
Thur	rest (due to racing at the weekend)	
Fri	am travel	pm 6 miles orienteering training: running in the terrain in Norway where she was due to race to familiarize herself with the map/terrain
		pm 3.5 miles hill run
Sat	am Norwegian selection race, short distance, 3.1km. 29min (5min down), losing 3min at the first control and a further 2 during the race due to lack of specific terrain running ability	
Sun	am Norwegian selection race, classic distance, 7.8km. 65min (3min down), losing 4min on one long leg due to poor route choice and not being aggressive enough	

Terrain runs were done in forests, with very little use of paths. While Yvette did not do much specific 'armchair' map work, in the later years she would use visualization in training, imagining she was racing (and beating) opponents.

controls. If you are worried about the lack of drinking opportunities, you might consider using a camel back or similar hydration system while running.

As with most off-road events it is worth being reasonably self-sufficient in terms of pre- and post-event fuel and fluid rather than relying on the race organizer or others to provide for you.

IF YOU WANT TO FIND OUT MORE

British Orienteering Federation, Riversdale, Dale Road North, Darley Dale, Matlock, Derbyshire, DE4 2HX.
Website: www.britishorienteering.org.uk
A Runners Pack is available.

CHAPTER TEN
Mountain Marathons

WHAT ARE MOUNTAIN MARATHONS?

Mountain marathons combine the ability to orienteer (navigation and route choice) with covering long distances on foot on two consecutive days in extreme, wild mountain surroundings. The first and original mountain marathon was held in 1968, established by orienteer Gerry Charnley and sponsored by Karrimor. The Karrimor International Mountain Marathon (or KIMM), which is still going strong, had two aims. First, to promote higher standards of navigation and safety for those who went into the hills on long expeditions by requiring orienteering-type skills to be applied to navigation in mountain

---

The Four Major Mountain Marathons in the UK

The KIMM can be held anywhere suitable and over the years has been held in the Lakes, Brecon Beacons, Pennines, Dartmoor and the Highlands (given the length of time it has been running, certain areas have been used more than once). The KIMM is held at the end of October each year (on the weekend the clocks go back), with both standard and score events. In the latter, competitors have a set time to score as many points as possible by visiting checkpoints, all of which have predetermined scores.

The Lowe Alpine Mountain Marathon (LAMM) is held in mid-June in Scotland over technical terrain. Compared to the others it tends to be held in wilder, more extreme areas, which lend themselves to more route choice. Checkpoints usually require fine navigation (that is, they are not obvious from 50m away) and may involve scrambling. The LAMM prides itself on trying to give runners a linear point-to-point course rather than just a circular route starting and finishing at the event centre. In recent years, this has meant competitors travelling by bus, boat or stream train to the start of their courses. The organizers of the LAMM go to great lengths to ensure that the venue for the race is kept secret as long as possible. The event centre is not revealed until the Thursday evening before the Saturday morning start (although broad guidelines are given in the race details). While not as popular in terms of numbers as the KIMM, many view the LAMM, with its smaller fields, more intricate navigation and route choice as the choice for purists.

The Saunders Lakeland Mountain Marathon is held in the Lake District or Cumbria in July. As well as the usual pairs classes, the Saunders also has a solo class, the Klets. A very pleasant additional extra for competitors is the provision of beer at the overnight camp!

The Mourne Mountain Marathon is held in mid-September in the Mourne Mountains, Northern Ireland.

There are also a number of long orienteering-type events, over one or more days, which can be useful preparation for mountain marathons, as well as being enjoyable in themselves. These include the New Chew Race, which includes a score class; the Capricorn, a 2-day event for solo runners and the OS Mountain Trial in the Lakes.

country. Secondly to make the event the toughest there was by being two consecutive marathons in length over mountains. While it is possible to do a mountain marathon without covering the complete marathon distance each day, this challenge still exists for the top classes.

While the KIMM remains the first and original mountain marathon, with around 3,000 competitors each year, at the time of writing there are three other well-known mountain marathons in the UK, in addition to others held in Europe. While each event has slight differences, the overall concept is the same.

COMPETITIONS

Mountain marathons take place over 2 days and are done in pairs (either same sex or mixed), who must stick together at all times. Each event has a number of different classes, based on ability. Courses are distance-based in that you have to cover a certain distance each day via a set order of checkpoints. The route that you take between checkpoints is, however, up to you and route planners will aim to ensure that there is no one obvious route between checkpoints (usually there is a balance between a shorter route with more climbing or a longer, more runnable one). Events are held at a different location each year to try to ensure that, where possible, competitors do not get the chance to recce the terrain prior to the race.

Runners are required to carry all they need for the 2 days. Each event has a mandatory kit list, all which has to be taken and will be checked when you register for the event (*see* later), as well as all the food you need for both days. You will therefore be competing carrying a rucksack weighing anything from around 4.0kg (8–9lb, for the top elite class runners), to 6.0kg (12lb, for the serious but not really skimpy) or upwards. The weight will obviously be slightly lower on day two as less food and cooking fuel is carried. Some races also allow you to throw your overnight rubbish away, which can often extend to include discarded day one socks, bubble wrap used instead of a sleeping mat or tin foil cooking tools. The LAMM, however, does not provide such facilities and all rubbish has to be carried the whole race.

Typical Distances/Times for Different Classes in a Mountain Marathon				
Class	KIMM distance	estimated winner's time	LAMM distance	estimated winner's time
elite	80km	11 hours	56km	12 hours
A	65km	10 hours	52km	11 hours
B	50km	9 hours	48km	10 hours
C	40km	8 hours	43km	9 hours
D			37km	8 hours/11 hours walking
novice			30km	8 hours
long score	7 hours day one, 6 hours day two			
medium score	6 hours day one, 5 hours day two			
short score	5 hours day one, 4 hours day two			

Distance/time = the cumulative distance and time for the 2 days.

The distance shown is the straight line distance between the checkpoints. You will invariably run further than this.

Choosing Your Partner

There are many factors which go towards 'enjoying' or achieving what you want from mountain marathons, perhaps the most critical of which is choosing your partner. First and foremost, it is important to pair up with someone who has a similar approach to the event as you. At the sharp end, teams will be doing all they can to win in terms of training, kit preparation, navigation and their mental approach to the race itself. Many others take part as a more personal challenge or for a good exhausting two days in the hills with a few other like-minded people. If, as a pair, you and your partner have different attitudes and goals for the event, this is not a good basis for a harmonious two days.

Next in importance is finding someone with reasonably similar running ability and fitness. Ideally, you should also be compatible over similar types of terrain. Having one strong uphill and one good at contouring and rocky ground limits the amount of time that as a pair you are both operating at optimal speed. One way of evening up the partnership is by the stronger partner carrying more of the weight, as often happens with mixed pairs.

It is pretty near certain that, whatever your ability, at some point during the event both of you will go through a bad patch (hopefully just not at the same time). When this happens the other needs to act accordingly and provide good support, not just running in front getting impatient. This might involve providing verbal encouragement, running with your partner (check whether your partner prefers you to run just in front as a windbreak, side-by-side, or behind), and making sure that your partner has eaten and drunk appropriately. It might also be worth taking some or all of your partner's load for a while. Remember, that if you have not already, it is very likely that at some point you will feel just as bad and want the support repaid. While

out on long training runs with your partner, it is worth discussing what type of support they prefer when going through a bad patch. For example, it is not helpful to be making lots of jokes because it would have cheered you up, if it just makes your partner feel worse.

It obviously helps if you both like and get on with each other. You will probably travel to the race together the day before and stay or camp overnight together. This is followed by spending two days and one night together when you will be tired, dirty and frequently cold, wet and hungry. It is worth thinking how you would react if you or your partner made a silly navigation mistake – would you still be happy to be with them? While it might sound like a potential for disaster in terms of friendship, many mountain marathon regulars compete year in year out with the same partner.

In theory, although it might seem ideal that both members of a team should be good at navigation and route choice, in practice it is not necessary. A number of the top teams work on the principle of one member doing all the navigation, the other being a 'pack horse' and carrying more of the weight. For most teams, a degree of dual input is used to find the way round the course. This may mean joint decisions on route choice and sharing navigation all the way round. Alternatively some teams take it in turns so that while one member is concentrating on navigating on the ground from checkpoint one to two the other is looking at the map to decide the best route from two to three. (Yes, the top teams can do this and run at the same time.)

Whatever you and your partner decide, what is important is that you do decide, and do so before the race starts. There is nothing worse than having massive arguments over who is doing the navigating during the race itself.

The Race

Most races allow registration either the night before or in the morning. Given that the race is likely to be held in a remote place, you could be starting as early as 8am in the morning, and there may be up to a 30min walk from the event centre to the start, it is worth registering the night before, if possible. On registration your kit will be checked and you will be given a small electronic tag. This is used to record that you have successfully found the checkpoints. As there are a number of different versions on the market, most races will have a practice control point at registration. It is worth taking advantage of this, as there is nothing worse than having a good day in the hills, finding all the checkpoints, only to find that your time has not been logged at any of them. Some races also have an old-style orienteering clip present at checkpoints for use by competitors in case their electronic tab does not work (*see also* Chapter 9).

The great advantage of electronic tagging is that it enables the organizers to know not only that you have been to all the checkpoints but also the time you arrived at each. This means they are able to provide post-race results listing the split times for all the teams – great to help work out where you made mistakes or whether your route choice was the best.

Race starts for mountain marathons are staggered, with teams going off at minute intervals. Some races have two teams per course starting at the same time. There will be people from other courses starting with you as well, so the temptation to follow others needs to be resisted: they may not be doing the same course as you, and even if they are, who is to say they know where they are going any better than you do? In the longer classes organizers usually start the women's and mixed teams first, with the top competitors going off at the back of the field.

Marking the Map

Once you start you will be provided with a map each. These are normally specially produced for the competition and use a 1:40,000 scale (2.5 cm = 1 km), with 10m or 15m contour lines. Standard Ordnance Survey maps are either 1:50,000 or 1:25,000 in scale. It is therefore worthwhile trying to do some pre-race navigation and route choice practice using either an old KIMM map or a Harvey's map, which are 1:40,000 (*see* Chapter 4).

In some events, such as the KIMM, each map is marked with the course number (A, Elite etc.), and the checkpoints and a straight-line route between each are also marked on. The maps are pre-laminated and come with the control descriptions written next to the section giving map symbol descriptions. Other events require you to write your controls onto your own map. Here, at the start of the race, you are given a map (often un-laminated, so remember a map-case) along with a piece of paper giving the controls, their grid reference and description. The first thing that competitors have to do is to mark the controls to be visited on to the map (preferably numbered to ensure you visit them in the right order).

Take as much time as needed to do this: less haste, more speed is certainly the key here. There is nothing worse than wrongly marking a checkpoint and then wasting time running to where you think it should be, then hunting around for it, only to find some time later you are in the wrong place. Unless one member of the team is near infallible in this task it is worth one of you reading out the grid references to the other who writes them on their map, roles are then reversed to check the checkpoints have all been marked in the right place. Once this has been confirmed the (hopefully) correct checkpoints can be copied onto the second map.

Some people prefer to mark only the first

checkpoint and mark the others up as they go along. This perhaps is best left to those with more experience as it is easier to make a mistake, especially if marking up while running.

When marking checkpoints, standard practice is to draw a small circle around the feature on or by which the control has been placed. It is important to draw your circle as neatly and accurately as possible, with the feature clearly visible in the middle and the circle not obscuring any other valuable features. One final point is to think about what colour pen you want to use to mark the controls: it needs to be one that stands out and does not blur into the map and the features on it.

A further variation is to be given a map with all the controls used in the event marked on. You have to identify which ones belong to your course from the control description and grid references provided.

Finally, depending on the event, you may (KIMM) or may not (LAMM) be given a second new map to use for the second day.

Once you have your map and it has been marked, it is a case of deciding which route you are going to take, visiting all the checkpoints in the correct order and making the overnight camp.

Overnight Camp

The overnight camp routine is an art in its own right. The sites for overnight camps are normally reasonably flat pieces of ground with a water supply near by, and no other facilities. Depending on the event all the classes may not camp together, with the A and elite classes often together, further away from the rest. In recent years the KIMM has provided portable toilets at some overnight camps, but do not expect such luxuries. It is just as likely to be a trench with a piece of tarpaulin around it (separate ones for men and women).

The first thing to do on arrival at the camp is get the tent up, ideally finding somewhere that is flat, not wet, out of the wind, not too far from water and not too near the toilets. The later you arrive the more unlikely you are to find such a pitch. Once the tent is up, get warm. Hopefully, you will be warm on arrival since you will have been moving all day, but on stopping it will not take long to chill off, especially in poor weather. Depending on the amount of clothing you have with you, this means either just adding as many layers as possible to what you are already wearing and hoping the damp will eventually dry off, or changing. If possible, put a dry layer on next to your skin. The final task is eating and drinking. This should start as soon as possible and continue for the rest of the afternoon and evening.

When going to sleep, be prepared to do so wearing pretty much all your clothing (except maybe your waterproofs), including, at times, hat and gloves. It is also worth drying gloves needed for day two by putting them in the sleeping bag with you overnight. While you might be able to get reasonably warm, you should be prepared for minimal sleep.

Day two is a repeat of day one, except starting from more uncomfortable and often colder surroundings and it is typically shorter. Most races commence with a chasing start. This involves the fastest pairs from each class going off first, followed at the appropriate time interval by those behind them for about 45 to 60min (this way, the first runner back to the finish is the winner). After this the remainder of the field start, either in a mass start or at timed intervals again. Getting ready to start day two is simple: wake up (the organizer usually sounds some sort of alarm), breakfast, take down the tent, pack rucksacks, change back into running gear and maybe eating or drinking, leaving just enough time to walk to the start for your start time. Warming up usually takes place on the first leg.

Finally, it is important to make maximum use of stops when you are running. Try therefore to combine stops. If, for example, you stop to check the map what else needs doing? Do you need to relieve yourself? Remove or

Route Planning in the KIMM.

add kit? Can you fill up your water bottle? This way you will minimize unnecessary stops and therefore 'wasted' time.

CLOTHING AND EQUIPMENT

For some mountain marathon veterans and serious contenders, getting their kit spot on

(this usually means as light as possible) is an art in itself and one that can take up considerable time, ingenuity and money. While there are undoubted benefits to be gained from having a lighter load to carry this needs to be offset by two things:

- Being very cold/and or not eating enough are likely to slow you down a lot more than

131

carrying that little bit extra bit of weight. They are both also potentially more dangerous, especially in bad weather.

- Fitness and navigational ability are both much more important for mountain marathon success than having a light rucksack and the latest gear. Your time and efforts should be allocated accordingly.

All mountain marathons have a compulsory kit list, and the box shows the KIMM requirements. Others are similar, the LAMM for example also requires you to have a piece of paper, a survival bag (not a space blanket) and stipulates certain first-aid items. The total weight for the top elite runners will come to around 4kg at the start of day one. For most runners it will be more than this, with around 6kg being reasonable (*see* box showing actual weights for two teams).

What does this mean in practice? When working out your kit and equipment require-ments remember that it is normally a compromise between comfort (and possible safety) and weight carried. This must be worked out individually, based on your personal requirements. Someone who feels the cold is likely to take additional clothes to put on at the overnight camp. Not doing so would mean being too cold to function optimally on the second day and thus running more slowly and making more mistakes.

Kit

Base Layer

Runners are required to have a pair of long tights, plus a thermal base layer and a thicker over layer. Remember you may well arrive at the overnight camp wearing the thermal top plus your waterproofs, both of which may be damp if not wet – is one other layer enough? Similarly, while it is possible to wear one pair of long leggings to run in and no others, this

---

KIMM Compulsory Kit List

All competitors must have the following minimum clothing (carried or worn):

- windproof/waterproof trousers;
- full leg cover additional to overtrousers, jeans not permitted;
- top and thicker fleece top, or equivalent specialized clothing (not cotton);
- anorak or cagoule which must have long sleeves and head covering;
- socks;
- adequate footwear with suitable grip for fell conditions – road running shoes are not suitable.

All competitors must have the following:

- head torch;
- whistle;
- compass – mobile phones and GPS systems are not allowed;

- map – as supplied;
- sleeping bag;
- emergency rations;
- first-aid equipment;
- biro or pencil;
- space blanket or large heavy-gauge polythene bag.

Each team must have the following between them:

- tent – it must be manufactured as a tent and not a bivi bag (you can use a bivi bag as a survival bag or a sleeping bag). The tent must be big enough for two people and should either have a sewn-in groundsheet, or one must be carried;
- food for the duration of the event;
- cooking equipment – including stove or solid-fuel blocks.

probably means being in damp gear overnight. Many runners wear a pair of shorts or knee length lycra tights to run in, putting long tights on at the camp.

Waterproofs

Check whether the kit regulations say you have to have waterproofs or whether Pertex-style windproofs are sufficient. Most runners go for a lightweight Gore-Tex or similar waterproof top. Remember that mountain marathons are renowned for bad weather.

Hat and Gloves

You lose around 30 per cent of your body heat from your head, so good headwear is vital. If you do not have a hood on your jacket, think about a waterproof hat or, alternatively, a balaclava. When deciding on gloves, remember that you will need to take food out of your pockets and use a compass while wearing them and that they will often be wet. Taking a lighter, spare pair, for the overnight camp is worth thinking about.

Socks

There are two things to consider here, trying to keep your feet warm while running (forget dry – one good stream crossing will see to that) and when at the overnight camp. For keeping feet warm when running the options are the same for fell running: either good wool-type socks or alternatives such as neoprene socks. For the overnight camp you need a second pair of socks and two foot-sized plastic bags. The LAMM provides specially made foot bags. Once you have changed and put on dry socks you then use the plastic bags whenever you need to put your trainers back on while in the camp.

Shoes

Fell or similar studded trail shoes are a must. When deciding what to wear, think about the terrain you are likely to be on: uneven, tussocky, rocky, steep, boggy and wet are all possibilities. If part of your feet or toes are susceptible to blisters, use zinc oxide or a similar product to tape them before you start

Overnight Camp at the KIMM.

and take some spare tape with you. After day one, all but the strongest tape will need repairing overnight.

Equipment

Tent
Here is where you can really start to save weight if you want to. There are a number of lightweight tents on the market which weigh around or just under 1.5kg (stripped down weight, without the stuff sack and so on). This can be further reduced by taking the minimum number of tent pegs and using rocks if needed. For those looking to go lightweight it is possible to get single-skin tents which weigh under 1kg, such as the Supair. The disadvantages are a more uncomfortable night due to condensation and/or less protection from the wind, plus if it is windy, cooking with certain fuels becomes more difficult.

Sleeping Bag
This is usually a straight compromise between weight and warmth. A number of companies make lightweight bags designed for mountain marathon use. These weigh around 600g. If going for a down-filled bag, it is worth putting it in a plastic bag (not the stuff sack), as well as your rucksack liner to make sure it does not get wet before the overnight camp. If it gets wet it will not keep you warm and means a heavier load the following day as feathers are notorious for 'holding' water. It is also possible to find bags with a waterproof outer.

Cooking Facilities
There are three options for cooking: gas, meths or solid-fuel blocks, each have their merits. Solid fuel tends to be lighter (depending on your cooking set-up) but more difficult to light and keep alight in the wind and takes longer to heat anything. Gas is probably the easiest to light, but the canister is heavy. It is worth spending time working out which set-up you prefer, not only in terms of fuel, but also the container that you will cook in, which will be influenced by what you plan to eat. For example if you plan to eat dried food, which just needs boiling water added, then, as long as you both have a plastic container to eat out of, you only need a small pan or equivalent (for example, a sweetcorn tin) to boil enough water for one or two people at

---

Key Cooking Tips

- Take enough waterproof matches and keep them in a small waterproof plastic bag.
- Check your cooking system works beforehand – it is not much fun having to try to 'borrow' fuel and so on from other competitors.
- A piece of tin foil can be used as a light-weight pan lid.
- If planning to use tin foil containers to cook in, make sure that they are packed so they do not rub together, otherwise you are likely to end up with a couple of sieves.
- Take a spare piece of tin foil to act as a wind-shield for the flame.
- Make sure you have enough fuel for all cooking sessions you plan, both evening and morning and that this takes into account the weather (it takes longer and therefore more fuel to boil a pan of water in the cold and wind compared to your kitchen).
- Think about how you are going to get the water from the source to the tent – possible alternatives are water bottles, camel back system, cooking pan, or a large plastic freezer bag (use the one you packed your sleeping bag in). Some runners take an empty wine box inner for this purpose;
- Cook in the tent with care: either setting the tent alight or spilling hot water are best avoided!

once. This saves on the need to wash up between courses, which in turn saves leaving the tent and getting cold. The alternative is to take one cooking pan and use that to eat out of, which is better if you plan to use fast-cooking spaghetti, for example.

Head Torch

This is one area where lightness is not a compromise. The small halogen head torches are not only lighter, but also last longer on one set of batteries and provide a much stronger beam compared to the older 'normal' ones. Ensure you have enough battery life.

First Aid Kit

The LAMM stipulates the minimum that you must take, although the KIMM does not. Most people usually go for plasters, blister patches, zinc oxide tape, a small bandage, a small wound dressing, antiseptic cream (a small amount in a plastic bag or wrapped in cling film), and ibuprofen. Other necessities might include an asthma inhaler or contact lens case.

Pen

Make sure it is waterproof if you have to mark checkpoints onto your map. It is also a good idea for you and your partner to take different colours, so if using the same map on both days you can avoid getting the checkpoints muddled up.

Luxuries

Many mountain marathon veterans have one small luxury that they take with then, despite the weight, to make things seem slightly more pleasant. Perhaps the most common are a miniature plastic bottle of whiskey or small airline toothbrush and paste. It really depends what you feel will make you feel that little bit better (or in the case of the whiskey, help you sleep).

Rucksack

A few years ago the choice of rucksack was limited, but now they are fashion items with companies making special ones for just about everything. The best ones for mountain marathons remain the reasonably simple ones, as these are lighter. Karrimor's 'KIMM' sac with a 35 litre capacity remains the market leader, although a number of other brands do similar products. When deciding what to buy there are a few points to consider.

- Size – how big?
- Pockets – do you want pockets in the waist band for easy access to food and so on?
- Mesh side pockets – do you need them for either keeping a water bottle in or food, if so are they the right height for you to access while on the move?
- Top pockets – do you need a pocket on the top?
- Camel back system – if you plan to use a camel back, is it compatible with the rucksack?
- Make sure it has both chest and waist straps and that you can get them secure with the rucksack full. Small people find that some rucksacks do not go tight enough, meaning that the rucksack will bounce around, Not only is this annoying, but also likely to result in it rubbing your back and possibly causing blisters, and will leave you with sorer shoulders.

Having a padded back to the rucksack is not so important, as careful packing will mean that the contents (either the tent, sleeping mat or sleeping bag) provide this without additional weight.

A degree of care should be taken when packing the rucksack, not only to make sure that it is comfortable and nothing is sticking into your back, but also so that the things you are likely to need first are on the top.

Sleeping Mat

While not a compulsory piece of kit, most runners will take something to sleep on, not just to provide a certain amount of softness, but also to provide additional warmth as well as helping to keep the tent contents dry (especially if you have a minimalist tent and sleeping bag). Your space blanket or bivi bag can also be used for this purpose (warmth and dryness) especially if you go for the traditional karrimat option – just make sure it is still usable for day two. Frequently used alternatives include bubble wrap or lightweight foam carpet underlay. If going for either of these two options it is worth taking one large piece between you and your partner. This can then cover the bottom of the tent (held down by rocks or bits of Velcro). It also means that both of you have something soft to pad the back of your rucksack – one has the tent, the other the 'bedding'.

Altimeter

These are allowed and can be useful, but only if you know how to use them.

TRAINING

As with other types of off-road running, being used to the terrain in which you will be competing is important. Running over knee-high tussocks for 8hr requires strength and agility. It is, however, very unlikely that you will be running the whole time. Most competitors, even at the top, will mix running and fast walking depending on the terrain and topology. Being able to walk strongly over really rough ground is often just as, if not more, important than running speed over better conditions.

One of the best ways to prepare for mountain marathons is to include long days or even weekends in the hills. The comfortable way of doing this is to use one base camp for both days, therefore not actually camping in the rough. Preferably, you should train with your event partner, carrying a rucksack and using a map of similar scale and style to that you will be racing with. These training days are not so much about running as quickly and as far as possible, but rather about making good use of your time and getting used to the map and the person you are running with.

Before you set out, select and mark a series

Suggested Order in Which to Pack the Rucksack

- Put a large plastic liner in the rucksack, into which everything goes.
- Place the tent or sleeping mat down the back of the rucksack, providing padding – make sure poles do not protrude.
- Put the sleeping bag, in a plastic bag, at the bottom.
- Follow this with the cooking equipment, plus overnight food and food for the following day (it is easiest to put food in separate food parcels).
- Add spare clothes (again in plastic bags or your foot bags) that you hope not to need until the camp.
- Put things you will need such as compass, pen

and drinking utensil into rucksack pockets along with food for day one – these should be accessible without having to take off your rucksack.

- Put the whistle, head torch, space blanket and first aid kit near the top of your bag, or in an internal pocket, so they are accessible if needed.
- Finally on the top, either inside or outside the bag liner, put your waterproofs, hat and gloves if you are not wearing them at the start. These can then be easily found and put on without getting the rest of the rucksack contents wet.

Kit per team	No	Elite team Total weight (g)	Notes	No	Normal team Total weight (g)	Notes
			Weights Carried by Two Different Teams			
trousers	2	0	worn	2	300	
overtrousers	2	200	windproof only	2	400	waterproof
thermal top	2	0	worn	4	300	spare for overnight camp
waterproof jacket	2	680		2	950	
fleece top	2	480		2	680	
socks (pair)	2	60	thin pair for tent	2	140	pair for tent
head torch	2	140	petzl zipka	2	140	petzl zipka
whistle & compass	2		carried	2		carried
food		2,110			2,825	
space blanket	2	60	cut down	2	110	normal size
map	2		as supplied	2		as supplied
sleeping bag	2	1,075		2	1,440	
rucksack	2	820	excess removed	2	1,500	
1st aid	2	60		2	100	
pen	2	15	waterproof	2	20	waterproof
tent	1	850	Supair	1	1,400	
stove	1	455	incl gas, pot, lid	1	600	incl fuel, pot, lid
sleep mat	2	170	foam carpet	2	300	foam carpet
hat & gloves	2	125		2	330	2 pairs of gloves each
poly bags	2	0	minimal	2	0	minimal
eating/drinking utensils	2	185	plastic spoon and Taste break pot, 1 water bottle	2	285	plastic spoon and Taste break pot, 2 water bottles
running long shorts	0	0		2	0	worn
total weight, day one		7,485			11,820	
total weight per person		3.7kg			5.9kg	

of checkpoints to visit. If you are using an old KIMM map, make up a course from those marked on the map. The checkpoints should not all be obvious things like trig points and summits, but include more intricate ones like stream sources, small crags and re-entrants. Working your way from one point to another will enable discussion over route choice. If there are enough of you, you may be able to compare the quickest lines, with different people going different ways.

As you run, get used to reading the map at the same time and make sure you know where you are on the map at all times. Practise making a note of landmarks on the map as you go past them – does the terrain around you look as you expected it to from the map? Use the time to work on your navigation techniques as outlined in Chapter 4. Finally, it goes without saying that this is also the time to practise your eating and drinking routine.

NUTRITION

Eating and drinking before, during and after a mountain marathon are important. The before and after requirements have been covered in Chapter 4. During the event there are three critical and inter-related things to consider:

- taking in energy while running;
- taking in fluid while running;
- refueling at the overnight camp.

Taking in Energy While Running

The first key consideration here is what to use: do you want to use solids (and if so, what?), liquids (in the form of energy drinks), or a mixture of both? The second consideration is how much, and how often? Ideally you should look to take in energy little and often, at least every hour or preferably every 30min whether you feel hungry or not. One way to

make sure that you and your partner take fuel on board regularly is to set your watch countdown to beep every 30min. Whenever you eat, it is a good habit to check with your partner whether they are also eating, this will remind you both to eat and drink. Less scientific and more open to 'bonking problems' is making sure that you use periods in the event when you are reduced to a walk to eat, for example when going uphill or when the terrain is really bad.

Ideally, you should be aiming to take on board up to 60g of carbohydrate per kg body weight per hour, or around 200 to 300kcal per hour. This is the maximum amount it is currently thought possible for the body to be able to use while exercising.

Whether you choose solids or liquid or both is down to personal preference. Some runners find that trying to eat solids while moving is not easy and they do not like the feeling of 'fullness' they provide and so they stick to energy drinks while running. Here, the best way is to pre-weight energy powder into small plastic bags. Depending on your race strategy these can then either:

- be emptied into your water bottle, filled up from a stream and drunk on the move;
- be emptied into a cup, filled from a stream and drunk in one go;
- be filled up with water at a stream and the liquid drunk with a straw directly from the bag.

Other runners prefer using solid forms of energy, finding that they feel hungry if they only use energy drinks. Typical foods include: jelly babies, energy bars, chocolate bars such as Milky Way, malt loaf, flapjacks, dried fruit, breakfast bars, Nutrigrain type bars, and fig rolls.

If using solid forms of energy make sure that you can reach them while on the move. This means using the waist-band pockets, the mesh pockets or an additional bumbag for storage.

Taking in Fluid While Running

Most runners use energy drinks while running, but as noted over there are different ways of taking on board fluid. The 'safest' method to ensure that you drink enough is to use either a camel back system or a water bottle (most should fit into the side mesh pocket of your rucksack) and aim to drink regularly from it. Relying only on stopping at streams for a mug or plastic bag full of water is more risky but is a tactic often used by the top teams.

How much to drink will depend on the weather conditions and whether or not you tend to sweat heavily. Drinking too much has the disadvantage in that you are likely to have to stop more often to relieve yourself, while too little could have an adverse affect on your performance. What is important is that once you arrive at the overnight camp you drink sufficient to make sure that you are passing a reasonable amount of pale-coloured urine.

Refuelling at the Overnight Camp

Refuelling needs to start as soon as possible, both to help replenish muscle glycogen stores and because something hot will help keep you warm. The box shows a typical eating pattern for a mountain marathon, including the camp meals. Teams will look to have three or four hot courses spread throughout the late afternoon and evening. Remember to take enough fuel to do this. Whatever you choose, it should be easy to cook (for example, just add water); quick to cook, as this will use less fuel; quite compact; easy to carry; filling and reasonably tasty.

Most runners' breakfasts tend to be based around oats, such as quick porridge, Ready Brek and so on, pre-prepared with added

Example Eating and Drinking Plan for a Mountain Marathon	
6 to 7am	pre-race breakfast and fluid top up
on the way to the start	energy bar, plus regular sips from water bottle
while running	two jelly babies plus mini-sized Mars bar or similar every hour; continual drinking from water bottle made up with 5 per cent solution
if hungry	carry 'spare' energy bar or similar to eat if start feeling hungry
arrival at camp	jaffa cakes and drink plenty of fluid while putting up tent; instant soup plus croutons with first boil of water
1 hour later	hot drink made with lemon-flavoured energy drink powder
30min later	main meal, for example noodles, quick-cook pasta (with packet soup for flavour), freeze-dried camping meals, snack pot or pot noodle type meals, mashed potato or potato flakes, followed by malt loaf and custard or rice pudding
before bed	hot chocolate
breakfast	instant porridge followed by a hot chocolate (if tight on fuel mix the two together)
last minute	if enough fuel a hot energy powder drink plus energy bar
while running	repeat of the above
at finish	plenty!

Runner Biography

Helene Diamantides is a member of a very select group of women: those who have won races out-right, beating all the men. Even within this group she is unique, having done so twice, once with running partner Martin Stone in the Welsh Dragon's Back (220 miles in 5 days) and again in the Western Isles Challenge, which involved running, cycling and canoeing.

After a varied career including teacher, professional runner (given up because she liked running too much to make it into a job), expedition leader, management trainee and building labourer, Helene retrained as a physiotherapist: 'the best decision I ever made'. She worked as a physiothera-pist for the UK athletics team at the Sydney Paralympics and at the time of writing is currently work-ing in Tasmania. 'I like the way I am not the only loony person and there are oodles of like-minded people to play with, the sun shines and new and interesting races to do'.

Helene was always sporty, running her first marathon 'illegally' at the age of sixteen in 4hr and

Helene (on the right) and Angela Mudge in the 1999 KIMM.

Helene Diamantides

25sec, despite the fact that she was meant to be training for 400m. Her background however was not restricted to running, and hockey, basketball, windsurfing, gymnastics, sailing, rock climbing and horse riding all get a mention. While at teacher training college she and a friend starting training together, which led to fell racing. 'First fell race was Fairfield, then I did the Yorkshire 3 Peaks Buttermere Sailbeck, then a Bob Graham Round. It was simply what everyone else was doing, so I did!'

Sponsorship from Reebok led to Helene and friend Alison setting a new record for the Everest Base camp to Kathmandu run, raising £5,000 for Intermediate Technology at the same time. Further sponsorship enabled Helene to do her first Mt Cameroon race in 1998. The gentleman concerned paid for Helene's ticket on the understanding that any money she won would go to pay his expenses first and then she could have the rest. 'I owe him my exciting running career and we have stayed in touch ever since'.

This career is varied to say the least, as even a brief look at Helene's sporting cv shows:

- Scottish mountain running team (World and European Trophies);
- Scottish cross country team;
- Great Britain 100km road running team (World and European Championships);
- twenty-two mountain marathons, including numerous top 8 finishes overall in the elite classes (needless to say being the first female or mixed team);
- fifteen yacht races (mixture of sailing around the British coast and running up fells);
- numerous adventure races worldwide (including the Eco-challenge);
- numerous other multi-day and high altitude races worldwide.

As a competitor over long, and particularly rough, terrain Helene has few equals and when she is fit few men, let alone any women, would find themselves in front of her. This is best exemplified by the 1999 KIMM, where she and partner Angela Mudge finished in the top 10 overall in the elite class. 'We took risks with our kit and both wanted to see how well we could do – it was a blast. We both like very weak tea so two bags did for two days – quite a saving in weight!'

For Helene, though, running is not just about winning, it is about enjoyment, rising to a challenge and having fun.

Typical Training

Monday	6 miles with club
Tuesday	track intervals
Wednesday	long slower run with club
Thursday	long reps or hill session
Friday	rest day
Saturday/Sunday	race and rest day or long run in the hills. In the build up to the KIMM this would include one or two long days out over a few weekends with a rucksack on Munro (Scottish mountains over 3,000ft) bagging.

Helene normally trains twice a day, with either a gentle 20 to 30min jog, cycle or swim before breakfast. 'I love getting up and out early – my favourite time of the day, it is not suitable for hard work so I just use it to air the brain'. If however 'I feel tired I do less and recover, if I feel unmotivated I make a real effort to team up with

continued overleaf

Runner Biography: Helene Diamantides *continued*

Helene's Top Tips

- Enjoy it – you do better if you do, if you are not enjoying it, stop and find something else!
- Nothing is impossible – the only difference between running 6 miles and 60 is wanting to.
- There is no substitute for preparation and hard work – who was it who said 'Good luck comes to those best prepared'?
- Running is good for the mental health – you can easily be the underdog on a bad day. There are no egos without a fall, certainly in hillrunning.
- I need goals – something fun to train and aim for that would be fun and a challenge. I suspect most people work the same way.

---

skimmed milk plus sugar, cinnamon or salt if required. Thus on the day it is just a matter of adding hot water, stirring and eating. For those who like a little crunch, consider mixing oats and muesli or granola-type cereal half and half or adding some dried fruit.

To make things easier, sort your food out as part of your pre-event organization. Put the food you need for breakfast, for the evening meal and for day two in separate plastic bags. These can then all be packed away until needed at the camp. Food for day one should be distributed around your rucksack for easy accessibility.

When thinking about how much food to take and what to take, it is worth heeding the advice from some of the top mountain marathon runners. Their view is not to skimp on food (other areas are better for weight saving), and to take something that you like as well. It is not uncommon to see packets of biscuits appear on arrival at the overnight camp.

IF YOU WANT TO KNOW MORE

Mike Parsons' *Adventure Race and KIMM news*: a free newsletter or 'ezine', available at www.kimm.com

Index